love letters
from
the civil war

For Cliff an old & cherished friend

D1226165

Edited by John B. & Donna L. Chapman

© 2000 First Printing
All rights reserved.

Sigler Printing & Publishing, Inc.
Ames, Iowa 50010-0887

The Library of Congress Catalog Card Number has been applied for.
ISBN Number

This work is dedicated first to my grandmother, Serepta Jane "Jennie" Coffin Cornelison, the daughter os William Coffin who with loving care preserved this portion of our family history and heritage.

I remember as a small child being fascinated with the brown walnut ox which was kept in the closet beneath the stairway which led upstairs to my bedroom. Grandma Cornelison would show me the letters in the box along with other Civil War memorabilia which had belonged to my Great Grandfather William Coffin. Although I was unaware at the time, but now looking back, I believe this is the point in my life that I became interested in the Civil War.

At her death the letters were passed along to my mother, Lavona Cornelison Chapman, the second person I wish to dedicate this work to.

She also with much diligence and care preserved them and through natural attrition they became my charge.

To these two very important people in my life I express eternal gratitude for their preservation of this portion of our heritage and in turn stirring an interest in me to continue this preservation.

And with special thanks to Bea VanFossen Smith. Without her enthusiastic support and direction we may not have completed our project.

JBC & DLC
Lander, Wyoming

TABLE OF CONTENTS

Introduction

On September 6, 1953 I married John B. Chapman who is the great grandson of William and Rachel Coffin. About a month later his grandmother, Jennie Cornelison, daughter of Wm and Rachel died. It was not long after that I became acquainted with the civil war letters written by Wm Coffin. They were kept in a handmade walnut box on the headboard of the guest bed in my mother-in-law's house.

John remembers that there was a closet under the stairway at his grandparents house in which there was a small chest filled with civil war memorabilia. He was aware of it all of the years he was growing up. He and his parents lived with his grandparents for a time when he was very small and later he lived there during the second world war and also for a time lived next door, spending much of his time with his grandparents.

After more then 20 years and 4 children we divorced and our lives moved in different directions. John married a woman who had a great interest in the civil war and she is the one who transcribed all of the letters and much more. She worked hard to cross reference and research the contents. Fern Murray Chapman made it much easier for us to prepare this work for publication. After her death in 1990 John and I found ourselves in a position to support each other and renew our relationship. By 1999 we agreed that it was time to come home to each other and make our committment to each other by marriage. We were married on September 22, 1999 just off the old Santa Fe Trail in Santa Fe, with my mother as our wittness.

It is with love and gratitude that we continue Fern's work and see this book published for others to share.

His mother Lavona Cornelison Chapman gave the letters to John. They are extraordinary due to accuracy of date, place and conditions. Also because young William was running his farm through letters from the war.

Before we begin with William it is important to note that in 1963 a Coffin family history was distributed to all descendants of Coffin family. In this history we learned some interesting things regarding the ancestors. Tristram Coffin came to America in 1642 and settled at Salisbury, Massachusetts. Early in 1660 in connection with nine other parties, two of whom were his sons, he purchased the Island of Nantucket, and resided there until his death in 1681. He was appointed Governor of Nantucket in 1671 and again in 1677. At this time, the spelling was changed from Coffyn to Coffin. (It was John Coffin, 8th child of Tristram and his wife Deborah were the branch of the family our family descends from. An earlier John, 2nd son that died.) We also learned that the home built by Jethro Coffin in 1686 is a point of interest at Nantucket and is furnished with the family things and is run by the Nantucket Historical Society. A book published in 1948 entitled "The Coffin Saga" written by Will Gardner was available at the time from the Whaling Museum, Nantucket Island, Massachusetts.

National Geographic magazine issue dated July 1984 has devoted much to the history of the Underground Railroad and escape from slavery. In this article are photos and story of Levi Coffin and his work. Levi was the son of Levi and Prudence Coffin. He and his wife Catherine Coffin were the Quakers who sheltered Eliza Harris, the fugitive slave woman mentioned by Harriet Beecher Stowe in Uncle Tom's Cabin, who crossed the Ohio River near Ripley Ohio with her babe on the floating cakes of ice. These people claim to have sheltered more than three thousand fugitive slaves during his life and never was caught with a slave in his possession, nor never told a lie to shield one. He visited family in Iowa a short time before the civil war. The National Geographic story, of course, includes all of the others involved in this endeavor. I am reporting from the Coffin family history here, although National Geographic confirms. After tracing this history we found that Levi Coffin, Jr. and William were second cousins.

William served with the 39th Iowa and was with Sherman in Georgia and Carolina campaigns and participated in the grand review at Washington and was mustered out June 5, 1865.

The safe keeping of these letters for 133 years speaks to the great love and respect for the people involved. They are still in excellent condition for their age and history. They are somewhat faded but the spelling and punctuation makes difficult some of the reading. We have chosen to keep them as they were written. In some cases there may be partial letters and Fern or John describe where they think they belong.

These letters are written with love for family and a Higher Power and have been kept in love - therefore we feel they are truly love letters. Enjoy!

Donna Lee Chapman

Note of Interest: Recently I was talking with my father and he told me some of our family history. One of the bits of trivia was that my great, great grandmother was a cousin of Robert E. Lee and she married my great great grandfather. Our family name was Griffin.

2

History of William and Rachel Coffin

William Coffin was born near New Lancaster, Madison Co., Indiana on 1-17-1835, the third child of Harvey Coffin and Rachel Mills.

The following was copied from an old clipping, from the Dallas County Record, printed at Adel, Dallas Co., Iowa, under date of September 11, 1917.

In connection with the observance last week of the sixtieth wedding anniversary of Mr. and Mrs. William Coffin, we are pleased to publish this week a photo of Mr. and Mrs. Coffin. There are not many couples, who are permitted to enjoy 60 years of married life, and especially with as clean and good record in every way as have Mr. And Mrs. Coffin. So far as we can ascertain there has never been a smirch on the good name of Coffin during the long period the family have been residents of Dallas Co., which is a record of which to be proud.

Recognizing the value of long and well lived lives, and the advance age to which these good people have attained, we wish to give a brief outline of their history leading up to the celebration so happily carried out last week.

Mr. Coffin was born in Wayne Co., Indiana (Genealogy gives he was born in Madison County, Indiana} on the 17th of January 1835. His parents were Hervey and Rachel (Mills) Coffin. The family moved to Iowa, in 1856, the father having before made three trips to the state to look for a location. He selected Jefferson Co., where he made his home, till the time of his death, which occurred in 1873.

William Coffin was one of a family of eleven children and was reared on the old home farm in Indiana, where as a boy he attended school in the primitive log schoolhouse, sitting on a slab bench and studying by the light from windows, covered with greased paper. He considered himself fortunate if he could attend school as much as three months in a year. When he was twenty-one years old, he came with his father to Iowa, locating first in Jefferson Co., and then in May of 1857 to Dallas Co. He settled on eighty acres of land in Adams Twp., which his father had entered from the Government the previous year.

After breaking twenty acres of the raw prairie, putting up hay for the winter, and getting logs to the mill, with which to build a house, he yoked his oxen and started to Jefferson Co., for his bride, who was a daughter of John and Malinda Shelley. They were married September 3, 1857, and a few days later started for their new home in Dallas Co, riding in a covered wagon, drawn by two yoke of oxen. Mr. Coffin made all the furniture they had in their first home, for more than a year, and it was several years before they were able to get store furniture of any consequence.

The privations and hardships of pioneer life were theirs, but their hearts were stout and their ambition exhaustless, which qualities brought them through all the trials of those days and enabled them to see the new country develop through the efforts of the hardy settlers.

The spring of 1858 was very wet, and not much wheat was raised, which made it necessary for them to live on corn bread most of that year. It was difficult to get grinding done, because the water was too high for the water wheels to run. There was one steam mill on Middle River, but as there was not a bridge in the county, it was impossible to get to it.

At one time they lived on young chicken, and new potatoes for three days. Not bad eating, perhaps you think, but when you have it for breakfast, dinner and supper for a few days, it gets old.

On the evening of December 11, 1861, while Mr. and Mrs. Coffin were away from home, their house was entirely burned to the ground, together with all their clothing, the winter's provisions, etc. Through the kindness of a neighbor, Wesley Krysher, they were allowed to move into his smokehouse. Mr. Coffin at once began getting out new logs to have sawed for lumber, for a new house, but the winter was so severe and the river frozen over so solid that no sawing could be done until spring.

On August 9th, 1862, Mr. Coffin and Mr. Krysher both enlisted to help fill the call for 300,000 men. Although his new house was not completed, Mr. Coffin moved into it to stay until he would leave for the Army, at which time his wife expected to go to her folks until his return. They had lived in the house eight days when it was struck by lightning and badly wrecked. The storm occurred at night and a young man named LeRoy McClellan was instantly killed. He had been making an evening call on a young lady, who was staying with the Coffin family, and when the storm came up he could not get home and the girl had made him, a pallet on the floor. He had enlisted and was expecting to go with the other men to the front.

The lightning moved the bed in which Mr. and Mrs. Coffin were sleeping several inches, but fortunately did not injure them. It broke all the dishes, but one saucer, which was quite a loss, as they had six plates, three cups and saucers and two or three milk crocks.

Soon after this, Mr. Coffin left for the camp at Fort Des Moines, and from thereon south. He was with Sherman on his March to the Sea, up through the Carolinas, and on to Washington, having part in the grand review on Pennsylvania Avenue.

After his discharge he was on the first train bringing soldiers to Iowa. He stopped a few days in Jefferson Co., where his wife and children had been staying, then on to Dallas Co., and home.

After the war, Mr. and Mrs. Coffin lived on the farm until 1881, when they moved to Adel. They lived here 7 years when because of the fact that their son, Henry, who had been living on the home place, had bought a farm of his own and they moved back to their first home. Some years later they again moved to Adel, where they have since lived.

Mr. and Mrs. Coffin were the parents of 6 children, whom, a boy and a girl, died in infancy; one daughter, who was Mrs. Ward Ruscher, was killed several years ago at a railroad crossing, in Adel; three are still living, the son .J. H., now living in Adel; and two daughters, Rachel M., the wife of Alonzo McNichols, in Madison Co., and Jennie who is now the wife of John Cornelison, of Adel.

Mr. and Mrs. Coffin are members of the Methodist Church, of which organization Mr. Coffin has been a Steward, for forty years. In politics he is a Republican, and is strictly opposed to the liquor traffic. He has held the office of Township Clerk, several terms and is a man worthy of any trust that may be placed in him, having every quality necessary for full, true patriotic and Christian citizenship.

Mr. and Mrs. Coffin are worthy exponents of the best there is in the life of the American citizen. Having seen the trials and sorrows, also the victories and joys of the early days, they are now enjoying the well-earned rest that comes to those who are faithful and energetic through the days of their pilgrimage. The early pioneer had many hardships, but also many blessings and the present generation owes much to the men and women who helped transform a wilderness into the glorious land which is ours today."

From "Past and Present of Dallas County, Iowa by Prof. R. F. Wood, published in 1907: the following is a part of the biographical sketch of William and Rachel L. Coffin:

" It was in August, 1862, that he felt the country needed his services and he responded to the call for three hundred thousand men, enlisting in Company C, Thirty-ninth Iowa Infantry. He continued with that regiment until the close of the war, being mustered out on the 5th of June 1865. He had proved himself a brave and loyal defender of his country, being always found at his post of duty whether it called him to the lonely picket line or stationed him in the heat of battle on the firing line.

During his absence Mrs. Coffin had been living with her people and also with his father's family. After his return from the war Mr. Coffin took her back to their farm and resided thereon until 1881, when he purchased town property in Adel and removed to the county seat, his son taking charge of the old homestead. Some years later, however, the son purchased a farm of his own, to which he removed and Mr. Coffin then returned to his old home place, where he remained for nine years. He then again came to Adel, where he has since lived in the enjoyment of a well earned rest. Those who read between the lines will gain a good idea of the life of diligence, perseverance and industry, which he has led. He has been unremitting in his labor and his capable management and perseverance brought him a measure of success which now enables him to live retired.

Unto Mr. and Mrs. Coffin were born six children, of whom three are yet living: James Henry, a resident farmer of Adams township; Rachel M., the wife of Alonzo McNichols, of Madison county, Iowa; and Miss Jennie, who is with her parents. The family are members of the Methodist Episcopal Church, in the work of which they are taking a deep interest, Mr. Coffin serving as one of the church stewards. In his political views he is a republican with prohibition tendencies, believing that the abolishment of the liquor traffic is the best solution to the temperance question. He has served for several terms as township trustee and in other local offices and in every relation of life in which he has been found he has ever been loyal to justice, truth and right. In early days his life was fraught with many hardships and at times, especially in the destruction of his home by fire and by lightning, it seemed that fate was against him, but he took heart and amid conditions that would utterly have discouraged many a less resolute man he continued on his way, his strong purpose at length winning a triumph over adversity. Wherever known he is held in highest esteem and is best liked where best known."

William and Rachel's children

James Henry, born 8/18/1858 Dallas County married Mary Jane King and Mrs. Samantha Harper.

Rachel Malinda, born 1/21/1860 Dallas County, married A.J.McNichols.

Ida Effie, born 10/11/1866, Dallas County - died 3/16/68 Dallas Co.

William Sherman, born 5/23/1869, Dallas County - died 9/13/70 Dallas Co.

Serepta Jane (Jennie) born 8/21/1871 Dallas County - married John G. Cornelison

Cora Lavona, born 4/21/1875, Dallas County - married Ward Rusher - died 2/11/1905

Daughter of Serepta Jane Coffin and John G. Cornelison was Cora Lavona Cornelison, born 6/23/1913 and married George Bradford Chapman 8/8/1932.

Only child of Lavona and Brad Chapman was John Bradford Chapman, born 6/21/1933 in Des Moines, Iowa and married Donna Lee Griffin, born 2/28/1935 in Kansas City, Kansas, on 9/6/1953 at Adel Methodist Church, Adel, Iowa.

Children of John Bradford Chapman and Donna Lee Griffin are:

Brad Frederick Chapman, born 4/6/54 - died 4/7/1954 - Des Moines, Iowa

John Bradford Chapman II, born 03/9/1956, Bremerhaven, Germany

Susan Kathleen Chapman, born 08/08/1957, Sedro Wooley, Washington, married David W. Ellis 4/19/1980 in Muscatine County, Iowa.

Amy Elizabeth Chapman, born 12/ 25/1959, Kirkland, Washington, married Micheal L. Saint Mary 11/13/1981 in Muscatine County, Iowa.

Matthew Jay Chapman, born 11/05/1963, Seattle, Washington

Children of Susan Kathleen and David Ellis are:

Jesse L. Ellis born 10/16/1980 - Iowa City, Iowa

Matthew A. Ellis born 06/05/1986 - Davenport, Iowa

Hannah L. C. Ellis born 04/20/1988 - Davenport, Iowa

Children of Amy Elizabeth and Michael Saint Mary are:

Benjamin John Saint Mary born 03/21/1982 - Iowa City, Iowa

Adam Michael Saint Mary born 08/25/1985 - Davenport, Iowa

Oct the 30th 1862
Camp Heron Iowa

Dear wife I this evening take my pen in hand to let you know that I am well at present   we started down here in about an hour after you left we got along fine that day while we could jump out and run when we got cold but after it got dark we dident do so wel though not as bad as you might suppose   we got to the railroad that night about 3 oclock and went in a barn and slept til day when we up and got our breakfast out in the brush and about 11 oclock we got on the cars for Devenport   we landed here that night about 8 oclock   our barracks is about one mile from the city   Davenport is quit a place   it is as large as severel such places as fairfield   there is another regiment here but they are expecting to leave every hour   it is about a mile from here to camp McClelen where severel of the boys from about Adel are quartered at present they are going to old regiments   Con Smith Sam Davidson Sam Edminson and severel others are there   this is Thursday just after dinner   had quit last night to go out on dress parade and this morning Oliver and Krysher and me went over the river to get some apples   we crossed on the railroad bridge   we war on rockiland   seen the house where old colonel Devenport was killed   we war in sight of the old fort on the island   we war through rockiland citty down to a big orchard where the man give us a peck of apples and we bought a peck for a dime and toddled for quarters   tired enough when we got back they war just starting out to drill   we went along and drilled til noon which mad me as tired as I have bin lately our regiment ant full yet cosequently we hant got our clothing & pay   we all drawed one blanket apiece and all the boys that want to can draw shoes today we have plenty of bed clothing to keep us warm almost any kind of wether O C Macy and me bunk together   Weir and Mat Mount bunk together   there is severel of our boys down with the measels but none that you are acquainted with   Bill Frank was better   the last account he hant left Desmoines yet   Oliver has got to be 5th Seargent   I dont know of any thing else that would interest you so I wil bring my letter to a close by requesting yo to write when you get the chance and tel me how you got home and what kind of a viset you had & C

direct your letters to

Wm. Coffin care of Capt Marsh co C

Camp Heron 37 Rgt Iowa volunteers

Camp Heron Nov the 28th 62

dear father   I now embrace the opportunity of writing a few lines in answer to thy very exceptable letter which I received yesterday   I was sorrow to hear of Luzenah bein so afflicted but I hope she is wel before this time   I am wel as comon   health is getting better in the regiment all the time   there was quite a serious accident happened this morning   there was a man from Co E that had bin on guard last night while out in line this morning to be dismissed put his foot in the hamer of his gun and let it slip off causing the gun to fire and shoot him through the arm close up to his sholder   it shattered the bone so the sergeans thought there was no chance to save his arm so they took it off there was a man died from Co E day before yesterday   it is the only death there has bin for some time   there is three of our boys that have lost their speech and I hear of some in other companyes in the same fix   some had the measels and some just had bad colds and got hoarse so the couldent speak above a whisper and when the cold left them it left them in that fix   I dont know what is the cause of it unless it is the dust   there is lots of dust in the barracks when the boys are makeing their beds and sweeping & C: I dont know whether they wil ever get so they talk or not   they are up and able for duty now but cant speak a word we war mustered in to the regiment last seconday and third day   we got one months wages and wee expected to get our bounty and premium before this time but it dident come yet   we didnt go through any examination when we war mustered in as was talked about   there wasent a man got off that came down here   if the regiment had have bin full to over- flowing I expect they would have looked at us pretty close but the regiment wasent full and the wanted all the men they could get. wel Luzenah wil frank come down a few days ago   he dident come til they sent after him he says it is stil very sickly up there   Manervy King died last Sunday with the dyptherea   two of Tom Jonses children has died   3 of Metses and Severel other children all with dyptherea   Netty Devenport is better   Tailer ant expected to live and old Johnnys little girl is very low   Levi Davis is getting up and about   Bill says Holingsworths are fixing our house up to move in to I dont know whether they aim to live there next summer or not   Anderson wrote that he had some notion of hauling a load of flour to you for me   would be glad if he could   I war down to town this morning and got a peck of meal and I expect to have a spot of mush for supper   I wish you was here to take supper with me   have some sausage and some beef to fry and I expect to have some milk and have a rite feast   we can by any thing here that we want to eat I generally aim to get some little extra every day   I dont intend to starve while there can be anything   had to eat   I make calculations to spend 3 dollars a month for extras if I want it   I think ten dollars wil keep you and the children and I dont aim to try to make money   I want to save enough to pay off what I owe   I guess I wont send you but 15 dollars this time   I want to buy a hat I

shal send what I send to fairfield by express   I wil write you a letter as soon
as I start it so you will know when to send after it   I wil send it to father   the
boys are in a great uproar about fixing to send their old clothes home   there is
a man from dallas that they are going to send by   dont expect to send any of
my old duds home now   we have to take it by turns a cooking and I wil save
my old coat and breeches to cook in we hired our cooks til this week   the
colonel said we must take it by turns so as all could learn to drill   my turn will
come next monday   we have to cook a week at a time   I rather dread it but
I guess I can do as wel as some others   I dont expect I wil get to come to
see you though I cant tel yet   I aim to come if I can get the chance   I sent
you a paper the other day   sent it to fairfield   the chaplain gives us papers
and little books to read once a week   I got a paper last Sunday and red it
through & I thought you would like to read it so I sent it to you you must get
the children a little book apiece and learn them to spell and read Jim Johnson
suprised Jo Early and got to be second corporal and it nearly killed Jo for he
thought more of his office than the colonel I must quit for this time and go our
on dress parade write often for it does me a heap of good to hear from you
tel all the connections I want them to write and I wil answer their letters let
all se this that want to no more
I remain as ever
Wm Coffin To all

Jan the 5th 63
Jackson Tenessee

Dear wife & children
I now seat my self for the purpose of writing you a few lines to let you know
that I am wel at present and hope these few lines wil find you wel there hant
bin any chance to send or get letters since we come down here on account of
the railroad being tore up   it was tore up & some bridge burnt the next day
after we got here   they have got it all fixed but about 12 miles we got a mail
last night for the first since we left Iowa   they run a coach across where the
track ant finished   we had a large mail destroyed when Trenton was taken by
the rebels   that was in a few days after we got here   our regiment was in the
battle at Parkers cross roads or red mound as some call it except our company we war lef up at huntington on picket through neglect of the officer of the
day or we would have bin in it to   we got in sight just as the yaller breeches
war making a blue streak   I hant found out what our loss was but not near as
heavy as the enemys   our regiment lost 3 killed and 40 wounded & there was
9 of our company give out on the road and was taken prisner there was 106
from the regiment give out and stoped and 102 of them war taken   Tommy
Ashton was driving a team and was taken   they are all parolled Zeke Davis
& hense Congar and Jo Early was taken   that is all that you knowed I stood

the marches as wel as any of them I never had better health in my life   we are liveing on what they call half rashens but we generally have all we want we camped the night after the battle on the field   saw severel dead men on both sides   we burried our dead and left the rebels for their friends to burry at their request we have been moveing so much that I cant hardly tel where all we have bin we have had pretty easy times except when we war marching which was just a week I dont know whether we wit stay here long or not we are very comfortably situated in little log cabbens built for the purpose this is a very pleasant place in the winter I dont know how it will be in the summer it looks as though people would starve out here before summer come the citizens of this place are on rashens the same as soldiers & they say there ant but 10 days rashens in the place they took from the rich and divided with the poor there is plenty in the country back a piece from town but there wont be long if they tare up the railroad much more for there is a good many soldiers here and they will have something to eat if the country affords it hant seen Krysher for over a week hes at Trenton he stayswith our things that we cant take with us on a march when we started we war at Trenton I left my blanket & shirt & drawers there I keep the old quilt it is better than a blanket I want you to write and let me know how you are getting along for I am very anxious to know write and let me know whether you got the money I sent you and how much you have on hand &C we dident get any the last pay day & it ant likely we wil if we stay down here it ant safe fore a man to try to come here with money I suppose you have bin some uneasy about me I wrote a letter to you 10 days ago but couldnt send it about the time they get the road fixed in one place they tare it up in another

There is apparently more to this letter .   It may have been lost and therefore not available .

This may be the addition to the 01-05 - 63 letter.

I got a letter last night from Jim Jones but he dident say any thing about you I Suppose there is nothing serious the matter as he would have rote   O C Macy got a letter from home stating old Ab Davenport had lost their baby and Steve vancleve was dead   tel your father we have some good bates of percimons which would make him think of old times if he was here   we get a little of almost every thing to eat   we ant choice   we take it as it comes we do our own baking now all together   sometimes we have meal & sometimes flour we have beef bacon pickle pork & bacon & once in a while a glorious mess of sweet potatoes   we ant bothered with pie pedlers like we was at Davenport we have over 300 prisners here they talk some of sending our regiment to Cairo with   we would like to get the job of guarding them through they are a motly looking set of fellows   they are all dressed wel enough but they have no uniform   there is narry two dressed alike   even the officers have no uniform   the privates we took seem to be very tired of fighting   they say it is bringing lots of f amilys to starvation   the most of them say they war pressed in to the serv-ice   I am on picket guard today   there is 16 of us together 4 watches at a time   the rest do what they please   I would rather be picket on than at camp there ant so much confusion & we have a nice place killing sheep   I hant seen any snow since I left Iowa   has bin cold enough to freeze a little 3 or 4 nights   I Wil quit for this time   I wont get to go in til tomorrow morning maybe I wil write some more then.

this the 6th.   we came in found the regiment in line ready take the cars Corrinth we wil start in a little while   we had a good time on picket last night we sent out & got a ham of meat & some sausage & corn meal and borrowed & oven and had the best supper & breakfast we have had in Tenessee.
I Wil have to quit for this time   write soon and tel me how you and the chil-dren are getting along   tel Dick to write   I allowed to write some to him this time if I hadent bin hurried off   so farewell for this time   direct your let-ters to Co C 39 Iowa inf Cairo Ill   that is the generel distributing office for all army mail matters
this from your affectionate husband
Wm Coffin

Jan the seventh

I dident get to put this in at Jackson & so I wil write a little more   we are at Corrinth Missisipi   we started about 10 oclock yesterday & landed at 10 last night   I think we wil be likely to stay here awhile the colonel says he is going to get large tents for us to day   I think that is some sign that they intend for us to stop awhile   things look the most like white folks lived here of any place we have bin at in dixey   its not a very .large town but what buildings there is are good ones   I must quit for this time and write a little to Dick   write soon for I want to hear from you often from your affectionate husband   wel Dick I thought I would try to write you a line though I dont know of any thing that wil interest you   I am in good health   I hope this wil find you enjoying the same   there is a heap of soldiers here but I hant had time to look around much to se if there was any body that I ever new or not   the 2 Iowa is here & they say there is one company from fairfield   I am going to their camp directly to se if I can find any acquaintances   the wether is nice as summer this morning   I must conclude for this time write soon and I wil try and do better next time   this from your   friend
Wm Coffin To R W Shelly

after noon
just received your letter & one from Dick & one from Jim Shortridge   they war wel   I read your letter without any trouble   I want you to write again tel Henry and MalindaI am glad they are trying to learn   I would be very glad to see you all tel henry pop hant killed any secesh yet but I seen severel that had bin killed   I want you to find out what regiment Jesse Williams belongs to and where he is   if he is any where very close here I want to go and se him we hant had any war news for a month to amount to any thing til today & hant had time to read that yet.   be sure and write
yours as ever

Camp Elliott   Corrinth Miss
Jan the 21   1863

Dear wife   I wil try to scratch you a line to let you know how I am getting along   I am wel as common & hope this wil find you & the children wel & doing wel   we have had a very disagreeable spel of weather for a week or more   last friday it snowed all day but mostly went off as it fell   about enough laid on to track a rabbit   Saturday I went out rabbit hunting but there was to many ahead of me so I dident get any   Saturday was pretty cold & Saturday night it froze hard enough to bare a man where there was stil water   old folks

14

that have lived here a long time say it was the coldest they ever saw it has bin rainy & cloudy all this week so far Weir is getting considerable better he can set up the most of the time he is stil in the hospital & ought to stay there sometime yet Krysher is on the mend slowly he is pretty sick but I think he wil get along we got word last evening that Ben Wadkins was dead he died at Jackson Tenessee I was over where the 2nd Iowa battery was camped this evening and saw severel boys from Adel that I was some acquainted with they are all fat and look harty but dock dodge he is as slim as ever & looks very natural they say they all had more or less sickness when they first came down here but now their are as harty a looking set of men as I ever saw Zeke Davis & Hense Cowger wasent taken prisner as I wrote before they war on ahead of the rest when the rebels come on them and they made their escape and got back to Trenton we hant drilled much since we left Davenport about all we do is to cook and eat and stand guard about every 3 days we hant had any male here til last night for about a week & not much then Jim Johnson got a letter last week stating that Sam Jones & nerve Long war married, I hope they wil do wel & have many little pleasures as they go along it is a 8 oclock at night & the drums is beating for roll call they call our band the wood-pecker band they lost all their drums but 2 in the fight & they sound about like a woodpecker on a hollow limb Wil frank Davenport is at Jackson sick he wants a discharge very bad I dont know whether he wil get it or not there has bin some discharged lately & there is a good many more that would like to be as for my part I find it no harder than I expected therefore I have noth-ing to complaine of I would like to be at home with you & the children very wel but I dident start out with the calculation of getting to do just as I would like to do so I calculate to be content with things as they come we dont get any news here about the war here I expeckt if peace was made we wouldent know it for 6 months the rebels stil keep tareing up the railroad track & cut-ting off our mail I wish they would burn every house within 20 miles of the road on each side nothing short of that wil even stop it I expect there is 20,000 soldiers guarding this road now now & stil they wil get in and tare it up, it is the citizens at the head of it & I would like for them to be furnished accordingly tel Henry & Sis I want them to learn their books & get so they can spel for me against I come home if I was allowed to I would like sende Henry a little rebel gun I have had severel chances to get guns that governe-ment has no use for but we ant allowed to send anything of the kind home the rebels have some mighty nice little shot guns they are very often just throwed round & broke by the soldiers I would be glad if you had some of the cotton I have seen going to wase I have seen lots of breastworks made of cotton bales I dont know of any thing more at present that would interest so I wil conclude write often dont be uneasy if you dont get letters regular from me I shal write whenever there is a chance to send them that may be often or it may not be just as it happens I cant tel when we wil get any money again some of the old regiments have bin paid this week but the new regiments dident

get any & I dont know when they wil   would like to get some before long   I
must quit for this time if   I was with you I could tell you a heap of things
that is hard to tel with the pen   tel all the connection to write as often as they
can   tel henry & sis I want to know what they are doing & how they getting
along   it is bed time so no more
this from your affectionate husband
Wm Coffin to R. L. Coffin & children

Corinth Mississipi
Jan the 26 1863

Dear wife I once more take my seat to write you a line to let you know that I
am wel and in good spirits yet I want to hear from you very bad   I hant
had any letters since about the 5th of this month I have wrote you severel   I
dont know whether you have got them or not   I sent one with a 20 dollar note
in on Oliver C Macy   I want you to write whether you got it or not
health is not very good in our regiment   there is a heap of sickness but few
deaths WeirCouch is discharged from the hespital but he ou;ht to have stayed
there some time yet.   I look for him to take a backset &   have to go back
there again   I dont look for him to ever get stout while he stays in the army
Krysher is pretty sick yet   he is mending slow   he's not out of danger yet I
think we have as good doctors as can be scared up anywhere or they would lot
more die than they do   I think there has bin pretty near half of the men in the
regiment under their care since we have bin here & there hant but one died yet
I never had better health in my life I have never missed a meal when there was
any thing to eat since I left Iowa   we just come in last night from ham burg
landing on the tenessee river   we went out to guard a train that went for provisions   hamburg is about 21 miles from here   we was 3 day we got to ride
as we went but we marched back   we had a very pleasant trip
hamburg has bin a rite nice little town but it is deserted except 3 or 4 familys.
            There is no business going on there   no soldiers stationed there
when a boat comes up there with supplies our forces send teams enough to haul
it rite away   there was 250 teams went as we did 2 50 Saturday & about as
many today   most all 6 mule teams. It looks as though we would have plenty for some time it take 3 regiments to guard train   it was reported that the
rebels war aiming to cut our train off but they dident undertake it   the country from here to hambur g is about like it is everywhere else   the more a man
owns of it the worse he is off there ant but four or five farms on the road that
any body lives on   the most of places the houses and fencing is all burnt   it
is nothing uncomon to lose big   orchards rite out in the comons The rebels
are a heap spunkyer than we are for if our country was destroyed lime theirs
is we would think we was ruined   you cant give any idea how it look down
here   every thing destroyed on all the main roads   back from the roads there

16

is something left after we get 15 or 20 miles from here I would give my farm for all Mississipi & be oblige to live here the peonle down here are as ignorant as Jackasses the negroes knows as much as the white folks that are here & they dont know enough to take them out very far and back again. wel Luzenah I have had my harecut & shaved this morning & washed up so that I think I look a little like a white man yet but I dont know whether I could act like one or not I got some peaches while I was gone I wish you & the children had some off them for I know you would like them especially if you had me to cook them for you . for I am one of the best cooks you ever saw I expect we have some things here that would be quite a rarity to you & you have things that would be a rarity to us It is raining today again we are tolerable comfortably situated here we are in large tents 14 in a tent we have a kind of furnace in ours which makes it warm enough and is a very good thing to cook on we have got a skillet & lid & we have some very good biscuits some times some of the boys make very good bread I hant tried making biscuits yet we use vinegar instead of sour milk we get about half of our bread stuff in crackers the rest meal & flour mostly flour we get plenty of sugar coffee & beans peas rice & a kind of stuff they call mixed vegetable which is very good, we live very wel when we draw full rations our lieutenant colonel that was wounded has got pretty near wel he come to the regiment day before yesterday he is the best officer we have Wil frank Davenport is said to be very sick not expected to get wel he is at Jackson Tenn in a post hospital I dont know of any thing more to write this time write soon and often for I want to hear from you as often as once a week when there is any chance there is some male comes every few days but not half as much as there ought to be no more at present his from
Wm Coffin to E. L. Coffin

I am going to send this to Cairo by our sutler and I think it wil go through if it gets that far this is 4 oclock in the evening raining hard all appeareance of a stormy night

Corrinth Miss
Feb the 17 1863

dear wife as it has bin severel days since I wrote to you I wil try to write a line I am wel as common & hope this wil find you all wel I have bin looking for a letter from you for some time but hant got any yet we have bin out on a tramp again we war down at burnsville after lumber it is about 16 miles from here it took us three days and a half to make the trip it is the awfulest road to team over in the world, we bridged one place for almost 2 miles it was an easy trip on us but it was death to the mules we camped the first night in about a mile of 200 rebel cavelry but they took good care to get

away before we got there   there was about a thousand of us & something over
100 teams   we camped in 5 miles of here last night   it rained nearly all night
it was the worst night we have ever bin out yet   Oliver & I done wel enough
we had a gum blanket that kept us dry   we run out of anything to eat so we
got some fresh pork and corn meal &   had a fine supper   we mad our mush
in an oyster can that we had to make coffee in & broiled our meat on a stick
and had a fine supper   dont you wish you had bin there to take supper with us
we war down in the piny regions   it looks very nice   the woods is as green
as summer   it is the first time we have bin where there was any pine timber
with the exception of the timber it is the poorest country I ever saw   I thought
I had seen some ornry country before but this beat it.   I was over to see
Krysher a little while ago   he is getting along very wel   health is getting better for the last 10 days   he got a letter from Frakes last night   they have nearly all bin sick for some time   Mary is very sick yet   Belles has lost 2 of their
children lately   Weir got a letter from Anderson stating that they was all well
as common   Ike Davis and Nan Caldwell is married   I dont know whether I
wrote it to you before or not   Will Davenport & Mcmullen come down last
friday night   Mcmullen was left at Cairo and wil was at Jackson Tenn   they
come to get their discharges   Will looks very bad   I dont think he wil ever
get wel if they keep him here much longer McMullen has the rheumatism
hudson harrison was burried last thursday   he made the 25th that has died in
the Regt all together and 5 five bin killed   there was 2 fellows deserted from
our co last Friday night but you wasent acquainted with them Wm Dillen July
Hills man deserted some 2 or 3 weeks ago they have heard that he was at home
all safe   tel granny I would like to see here and talk with her about things   I
expect that things down here look a goodeal like they do where she was raised
tel Henry & malinday I would like to se them and hear them hollow pop & I
hope it wont be long til this war wil be over so we can all go home to look at
the country   every where we have bin it looks as though they couldent stand
it much longer   the fences are nearly all destroyed where ever there has bin
any to destroy   rails make a nice fire to lay by   I expect we used 5,000 to
bridge that swamp and burnt twice as many   think that is about as good way
as we can whip them   if we burn their rails they cant raise stuff to support the
war   the citizens say they are very tired of it   some say they are bound to
starve   if the war lasts 3 months longer others Feb. say they can fight us 7
years yet   I think they are whiped now if they would only say so   tel
Williamses folk If you see them that I hant seen jim since I wrote to Nathan
I allowed to go over to their camp last Sunday if we hadent have bin ordered
away with the train   we are assigned to this fort and I expect we wil not leave
here for any length of time soon   we may go out on a scout or something of
that kind but I guess this wil be our home   I would rather be any where else
I have seen   this is a very nice but there is to many ded man & horses &
mules around here to suit me   It is almost imposible to get any good water here
now & in the summer it wil be worse   there are hundreds of men burried here

that ant a foot under the ground   I saw where a rebel was burried the other day   he had bin killed in the battle   there had bin some dirt throwed over him just as he laid.   I must quit for this time for I dont expect what I have rote wit interest you much but you must excuse me for couldent think of anything to write   I want you to write as often as once a week for I like to hear from you and the children often
this from your affectionate husband
Wm Coffin to R L Coffin

March the 6th 63

Dear wife   it is with pleasure that I take my set to write you a few lines to let you know that I am wel as comon   hope this wil find you all wel   health is getting a little better than it was a few weeks ago   stil there is severel sick Weir is stil mending slowly   krysher is not so wel   the white swelling is comeing back on his leg which pains him considerably   Weir got a letter from Anderson last night stating that they war all wel   it give an account of the death of Belleses wife   it appear as though every-body up there is going to die   unkle Middletons was down the Sunday before and said they war all wel on north coon   I seen the neatest piece of rebel work yesterday I have seen since I come south   it was a shoe made the upper of leather and the sole was wood   there was insole and out sole with heal tab abut on the out sole   it was a very nice shaped shoe - but I dont expect there would be much spring about it   it was put together with small screws and was water proof I have to give them credit for being sharper than I had took them to be.   the negro that had it said that necesity had learnt the rebel to do lots of things that they had never thought of before wel we have butter this week for the first since we left home   we sold our extra coffee to get it we get 35 cts for coffee and give 40 for butter we pay all our soda and pepper with coffee   the butter we get is northern butter   we can get southern butter for 35 cts a pound but we wont eat it   it is mostly funky stuff   I dont know any thing about our money yet   wrote to Anderson to send you all he can he wil be apt to send you some if he hadent sold the wheat and paid out the money before he got my letter he hadent rented the place yet   I got a new pair of shoes night before last   is the first new clothing I have had since I left Iowa   we can draw clothing twice a week if we want any   then all we have to do is to tel our Captain and he wil get it   tel the children they must be good children and not be saucy to folkes   must quit for this time write soon and oftener
this from your affectionate husband
Wm Coffin to Rachel L. Coffin

wel father   I went over and seen unkle Jonathan this morning he is tolerable wel   said he got a letter from aunt Phebe night before last   they was wel her last office address isWinterset Madison Co.   he says he thinks he will write thee a letter soon   he says he dont have much time to write which I know to be the case we dont any of us have so powerful much surplus time since there has bin so many sick.   they still fetch in a few that tern up   occasionally they fetched in about a hundred the other night there is deserters from the rebel army comeing in here every few days   a good many of them join our army rite away   they all say that there is lots more that would like to get away no more   Wm. Coffin.

Tuesday   March the 10th /63

Dear wife   it is with pleasure that I take my pen for the purpose of writing you a few lines   I am wel with the exception of a cold   I hope this wil find you and the children wel   we have had a goodeal of rain lately   it rained hard nearly all night last night and looks as though it wasent over yet   we had the hardest hail storm last Sunday evening I ever saw   there was lots of hail as large as a prairie chicken egg and the ground was completely covered with hail   it rains for keeps when it does rain lately we hant had any cold weather for some time   health is stil improveing some in our regt   Weir Couch is getting pretty stout Krysher is confined to the hospital with his leg   I have my doubts about him ever being able to do duty as a (------------) W F Davenport is getting better and I think he will get wel I am cooking this week it dont suit me very wel   it is to confineing   we cook in our tents yet but wil have cook sheds by the last of this week   we got word that all the prisners from this regt war exchanged and on their way here   there is about 150 of them which wil help the looks of our regt considerable   I guess there is some of them that would rather been excused from comeing back   · we hant got any money yet & I guess it is uncertain about us getting any soon   I want you to write and let me know how you are getting along   I hope Anderson wil send you some money I hant heard yet what he has done in regard to the wheat and corn I want you to write and let me know what you have concluded to do about keeping house and all about it   if you stil want to keep house wil try to make some arrangement to get you some money to fix up with   tel Williamses folks if you see them that I was over to Jess last Saturday and he was wel and hearty   he looks about as wel as he ever did   Tel Henry & Sis I would like to see them and tumble them around while   tel them they must learn their books so that they can spe for me when I come home   I feel in hope this war wont last much longer   the prospect is that they wil have vicksburg in a few weeks at farthest and when that is done I think they wil feel their holts slip pretty fast   there is lots of   (--------) here that that wil have (-------- --) starve or eat weeds before long   wel I must quit and go to getting dinner after dinner and I wil try to finish my letter   it is raining some and looks like being a rainy time   I hant had any letters since yours of the 11 of feb only

20

fathers of the 21   I begin to want to get some letters pretty bad   we dident
get any mail last night and I dont expect we wil for 2 or 3 days on account of
the railroad being damaged by water between Jackson and Columbus   Our
regiment hant bin away from here in a good while hope we wont have to make
any trip til it quit raining there is some kinds of bushes that are getting pretty
green here now and the grass is begining to start up considerable   I have saw
peas where they have scattered around camp up 2 or 3 inches   I guess that if
they war let alone we could have green peas in a month or 6 weeks   I dont
know of any thing more that wil interest you so I wil bring my letter a close by
requesting you to write often   I would be glad if you would write as often as
once a week any how and and oftener when you can I never get tired of reading letters no more
yours as ever
Wm Coffin to R. L. Coffin & C

wel father and mother as I have a little paper left I will try to write you a few
lines though I hardly know what to write I have a bad cold which makes my
head rather thick to rite   health is very good about this place except in the
new regiment   they stil have considerable of sickness though it is getting better   I think the hard rains we have had lately wil improve the health the coming season as it is washing away a heap of filth that has accumulated around
here   we are getting along very wel lately we have about enough to do for
good exercise   nothing but what any wel person can stand   I wil quit quit
as   I   ant   in   much   of   humor   for   writing   write   often
this from your affectionate son
Wm Coffin

Saturday   march the 14th 1863

Dear wife   I now take my pen for the purpose of trying to write you a few lines
I am wel as comon and hope this wil find you and the children wel   I received
the letter you and mother rote mailed the 4th last night and was glad to hear
from you for it had bin a good while since I had heard from you   I also got
one from Yhol & Jeremiah   we hadent had any mail for severel days til last
night   you wrote that you dident get letters as regular as you ought to   I rite
as often as once a week and the most of the time oftener   I have answered all
the letters I have got   I have got 4 letters from you   I want you to write as
often as you can and some of them wil get here   you must take things as
pacient as posible and not get discouraged   there is no telling when this war
wil close but I hope it wont be long   The rebels are whiped now   if they
would only say so   You rote you wanted me to get a furlow and come home

that is a thing a wel man cant do   it is very seldom a sick man can get a fur-low anymore   I hope never to get sick enough to get a furlow   not that I dont want to see you but a man has got to be sick 3 or 4 months before he can get a furlow I hope never to be sick   I am the only man in our company now but what has bin sick more or less   I have took all the care of my self the cir-cumstances would admit of and stil expect to as long as I stay in the service and that is a thing a great many soldiers dont do they eat all kinds of trash and lay down on the ground to rest when they are tired and warm   tel henry and sis I would like to se them and have a big play with them   tel henry he musend run them old hens to much or they wont lay for him   tel him I want him to send me some eggs   they are a scarce article down here the soldiers have killed all the chickens in 20 miles this place   eggs are 25 cts a dozen in Corinth butter 40 cts per lb   there is citizens mooveing in here every day to get some-thing to eat   they are starveing out   there was some came in yesterday from Alabama they say there has bin some starve to death down there   that looks pretty hard but that is what we wil have to fetch them to before they wil behave there was two familys come in from pitsburg landing yesterday   there was 2 woman and six or seven children   the children was barefooted   they had one old horse no wagon so you can imagine how distressed they looked   wel grany I would like to see the   I think I could interest the awhile telling what I have seen down here although I hant seen any thing to what some have   I am glad to hear that the keeps thy health as wel as the does   we have had very nice weather here for a few days   it is just about warm enough to be comfortable without a coat on   when it is nice weather here it is very nice and when it rains it is as much the other way   wel Luzenah I was sorrow to hear of you have-ing the bellyacke but I am glad it was nothing worse I hope you wil be all rite before you get this   I hant had any letters from dallas since I rote before   the boys in our company are getting along tolerable wed now Cal Hill had a chill this morning   I dont know whether it wil get him down or not   he is so fat he cant hardly see Oliver Macy is a getting as big bellied as some old woman krysher is getting better he can walk around some   Bill frank dont gain much he is very homesick which is the worst sickness a soldier ever gets   must bring my letter to a close and get dinner   my time wil be out in the morning and I will be glad you bet this
from your affectionate husband
Wm Coffin to Rachel L Coffin

After dinner and I wil rite a little more   it takes me about 3/4 of the time to do the cooking   I have 411 to cook for   we take it week about cooking   our boys that we left scattered around when we first came South have all got here at last   only Tom vancleave he is at Jackson   he has had the sore eyes very bad   I guess he wil get a discharge   I got a new pair of pants the other day their are first rate pants and I got a pair of drawers which wit make clothes enough to last me this summer   the most of the boys drawed hats but I dident

like the hats that they drawed so I dident get any   I am going to buy one if we ever get any money   I want you to keep yourself & the children wel clothed as long as you have any thing do it with and I hope that wil be as long as I am away although it looks like a slim chance for money now   I feel in hopes that Anderson wil get some money for that wheat or corn and send to you   I dont expect we wil get any here til the first of May   I must bring my scribling to a close   write often for I am always glad to get a letter from you   you need not be uneasy about me reading them for I can read them without any trouble this from your affectionate husband as ever
Wm Coffin to Rachel L. Coffin

Camp Elliot   Corinth Miss
March the 19th   1863

Dear wife   I now take my pen to write you a line   I am about as wel as comon I have had the diarhea last night and today which makes me feel a little funy though I think I wil have it stoped soon   I received your leter of the sixth and was glad to hear that you and the children war as wel as you was   this is a very pleasant day   it look like rain   you wanted to know about the cow   Anderson got her and Weir is to pay me the first time he get any pay from goverment we dont know yet when we wil get any pay   health in our Regt is improveing considerable W F Davenport is the only man in our company that is much sick now George W Case died yesterday with an apopleptic fit   I guess you dident know him   he lived close to vanmeters mill he was a young man and a first rate fellow we have lost 7 men out of our company since we left Iowa but I hope we wont lose any more soon   we are getting better fixed all the time to take care of our selves tel granny that it ant ticks that bothers us it is boddy lice we call them graybacks   they are about as large as a grain of wheat they lay their nits in our clothes and that is the reason we have to change often   I dident mean for you to understand from what I wrote about taking things easy that I dont want to see you   I would be as glad to see you and the children as any body could be but I know there is no chance at present and so I take every thing just as easy as posible   there is some that are dissatisfiedat every thing that is done   I aim to do my duty as a soldier as long as I am a soldier   I must quit for the present and go to the burying

Just come back and I wil try to write a little more tel Sis she must be a good girl when she goes to meeting and not cut up so or I wont let her feel my tittys when I come home   I expect they are getting pretty bad spoilt liveing about at so many places   you must keep them as near strate as you can   tel henry he musent worry them old hens to bad   I would like to se his tohead waddleing around after them   I recon he ant as fraid of a hen as he was when that old hen come so near scaring him to death in the oats stack   tel granny I am glad that she is able to read the news   I hope she wil enjoy herself wel at it   I have a good chance to get the news but I dont take much pains to keep myself posted   the excitement about the war ant half as high here as it is in the north here they dont think of anything but to whip the rebels and in the north they have war matters and politick mixed   no more   yours as ever

Note : This letter was in the same envelopee but had no date.)

Respected father   as I have bin writing some to Luzenah   I wil try write thee a few lines   we are getting along tolerable wel at present and I believe generally in good spirits though there are a few that would rather be excused from the service I feel in hopes we wil be able to bring the rebels to tow before long if we get vicksburg I think we wil make a short thing of it an I believe we wil have vicksburg before long   I hope you wit quite the copperheads up north if they dont quite with their own accord   there has bin three men arrested in Dallas for expressin their treasonable sentiments   I do hope they wil punish them to the full extent of the law   if the deserve hanging I say hang them   I can have a little feeling for a rebel in the rebel army but I could se a copperhead hung with a good grace   this thing of us haveing to stay down here 3 or 4 months longer than we need to if it wasent for them dont set set with the Soldiers   wel I wil quit for I am out of anything to write about   write when ever the can conveniently no more

from Wm Coffin   wel mother   I am glad to hear that the and Luzenah has as good times as you do   I hope you wil get along wel as long as she stays there I would like to have seen henrywith his new jacket and gallases on for I expect he felt petty large for he feals as large as comon boys of his size in a generel way and I expect his new clothes swelled him a little larger   you needent to have sent the ink powders I can get ink here now   there was a while that we couldent get any but we can get plenty now   I wil quit for this time write often Wm coffin

Corinth   March the 22

Dear wife   as it is Sunday evening and I have a little leasure time I wil write you a few lines   I am wel as comon and I do sincerely hope this wil find you and the children wel   the health of our camp is getting tolerable good   there is none of our company that is much sick at present but Will frank Davenport he is stil pretty low and guess he wont ever be any other way while he lives unless he gets to go home   he wil get a discharge I guess   he is looking for

John Y down after him   Stephen Adam from dallas he is here now   he come to see Ellick Logon.his brother in law   he says the copperhead are cutting a tolerable big stiff up there   he says they ant as bad as they war a while back he says it was reported that a few days before he left that lum franklin had said that he was ready any time to go at the head of a company to destroy union soldiers property   he says he wouldent be surprised if he dies trying to pull a limb off of a tree before long   Old Chance and Lem war both arrested for their treasonable gab but they got copperheads enough to wear them out of it   I wish they had have hung them   Aaron Leverton was arrested the same time and was released by using the same game   we have very nice weather lately which makes the appearance of the camp much better   we have plenty to eat and plenty to do to make it digest right and plenty to wear and the boys generally in good spirits which makes a good time generally   wel I was over at the negro corell this afternoon to meeting and to see some of the darkeys get married there was 16 couples more or less got married   they formed a circle and war all married at once   them that have bin married when they war slaves have to get married again on account of them haveing no certificates from their masters to show that they ever war married   I hant had a letter from Anderson for a good while   I dont know what he has done with my place yet   have never heard how our sheep done this season   I guess I wont be likely to get any from Belles as he has had so much bad luck   I expect he is about once through and I shant crowed him if never get what he owes me   I guess there is a prospect of John Y Davenport and Mary Hickumbottom getting married, a likly prospect ant it,   I wil quit for tonight as it is getting dark for I wat to go to prayer meeting to night

this is monday morning and I wil try to write a little more   it is raining some this morning   Weir Oliver and I got a letter in partnership from Meshack Couch last knight   they war wel except Hanah   she has another girl not very old   she is getting along very wel   they send their love to you   Krysher is discharged from the hospital and come back to camp   he ant very stout he is getting along very wel Matt Mount is in the hospital with the sore eyes   sore eyes are very bad in our regiment

(Note: This letter has no date. It was probably written between 03/22/1863 & 03/30/1863

wel luzenah   as I have bin writing some to father and mother I wil try and write you a few lines though I hardly know what to write as there has nothing new transpired since I rote before   I stil have my health very wel and I hope this wil find you and the children wel   I should like to be with you today as it is a very rainy day and I know you miss one more of wet days then any other time Krysher is mending slowly   he is going to be a good while getting stout W

F Davenport is about like he was when I rote before unless he get a discharge soon I dont think he wil live long   if he could get home he might get wel   Wm Mcmullen wil get a discharge soon   I guess we shal look for our men that was taken prisner in a few days   they are exchanged and ordered back   William writes that he was taken prisner and took the oath but I guess they wil fetch him back if he dont slope   I hant never heard any thing about our sheep   how they are doing or any thing concerning them   I suppose they are all rite or I would have heard something about them   Mary Caldwel is dead   she died lately   I dident hear just when   dock Rickinson got it last night in a letter she died with the consumption dypthery and tiphoid fever is stil raging considerable on Panther creek   Jim Johnsons father is discharged and and at home by this time he was in the same Regt same company that Jonathan Williams is he had bin sick the most of the time since he enlisted Jim has bin on the sick list for the last 2 months   he looks wel but I dont know how he feels   he tried to get a discharge but failed   he is getting better now it is stil a raining like Sam hill I am mity glad we dident go out after chickens for all I would have got wouldent have paid for me for going through the rain   the guards generally aim to get one apiece and that wouldent near pay for marching all day through as cold a rain as this is   tel granny I would like to se her very wel and talk with her while she smoked her pipe   tel her I weigh 173 lbs   that is as much as I ever weighed so she may know I get something to eat and enough exercise to make it digest wel they have put us through pretty regular drilling for 2 or 3 week   we drill 4 hours a day when it is nice weather which is better for a persons health than to do nothing   then we have to go about a mile and a half and cut our wood and get it hauled which is considerable job   then we have to wash as often as once a week or the graybacks would carry us off   they dont bother us much if we keep clean   but if we wear our clothes til they get dirty they wil breed natural almost   Louis macy wrote to me that he wanted to put all my stalk ground and sod in wheat & oats   he offers one fourth in the bushel   I shal give anderson orders to let him have it   I would rather do that than to have somebody in the house tareing up jack I guess Anderson wil tend the ballance.   I recon alltogether it wil pay the taxes and that is as good as I expected when I left it I must conclude this
from your affectionate husband
William Coffin To Rachel L Coffin

write to me about what you think about keeping house and and I wil make the raise if I can and I think I can   I think we wil get some pay the last of this month   write often for I want to hear from you often

March the (Between the 22nd & 30th) 1863

Note: The envelope is postmarked Apr 8

Dear wife   I received your letter of the 14th last knight   I am sorrow to hear that the children was sick and you in such poor health   I hope before you get this you wil all be wel or better at any rate   I would be glad if I could be there to help you wait on the children for I know that you have a hard time I am wel as common at present and we are getting along very wel as a generel thing   we hant got any money yet   I got a letter night before last stating that he war going to send you some pretty soon   he wil send you all the wheat fetches which wil be enough to do you a while tel granny I was sorry to hear of her being so unwel but hope she wil be better before long   it rained nealy all day yesterday and day before   today it is clear and tolerable cool   the coldest it has bin for some time though   not cold enough to frost any   things begin to look pretty grean down here   now the grass is coming on considerable and other things in proportion   I want you to write often and let me know stil how you are getting along   I guess I get the most of your letters but some times they are a good while comeing   I write to you as often as once a week all the time and generally oftener

I remain yours as ever to

R L Coffin from W. Coffin

wel father I wil try write the a few lines though I dont feel like as though I had any thing to write about   health is getting tolerable good here to what it was I hope this wil find thee in better health than the was when the rote   got a letter from Jim and Sarah last night   they war wel when they rote   Sarah writes that she is going to start home in 2 or 3 weeks   she writes she is going to stay 5 months   I suppose you have heard the arrangement before now   I dont get any news from any of the mills boys   uncle henry requested me to write to him and said he would answer it   I wrote to him when we first come to Jackson but have never got any answer   unkle Jonathan is wel   I have never heard him say whether he has rote the yet or not   I dont think of any thing more at present so I wil conclude for this time this from thy affectionate son

Wm Coffin

Luzenah you needent pay the doctor bill til I send you money   you wil probably need all the money you can get for other purposes before I get any   I wil quit for this time and try and do better next time

from your affectionate husband

Wm Coffin To R L Coffin

Corinth Miss   March the 30th   63

Dear wife   it is with pleasure that I embrace the present opportunity of writing you a few lines in answer to your letters of the 17th and 19th which I received last Saturday   I was glad to hear that you was getting along as wel as you was   I was very uneasy about the children til I got your letters stating that they was better   I hope by the time you get this you wil all be wel   I am wel with the eception of cold   I have bad cold but think I wil be as wel as ever   it has bin very cool here for 2 days   health is tolerable good except cold there is a good many complaining with colds   Krysher is getting pretty stout again   his leg hurts him some yet but I guess they wil get it cured without it getting very bad   Anderson writes that he has severel chances to rent our place by letting them moove in the house   I dident want any body in the house but rote to him if he could rent it rite to do so   Lous Macy is to take 25 acres for wheat & oats   they have bin sowing some of it already   Dave Clark and jack Franklin 3 of neals boys Jake Carter and a great many more from about there are going to the peak   some of them have allready started they are mostly running from the draft   I hope they wil stop the poor cowardly cubs and make them stay at home or come in to the army   they ort to be ashamed to of themselves as long as they live but I expect they are scared til they dont know w hich end is up   You can do as you please about going to writing school   I would like very wel for you to learn to write better but I can read your letters without any trouble   you said you would like to se me cook and eat with me   I expect I could get a meals victuals that you could eat very wel   I cooked a mess of greens last night and I know you would like to have had some of them   we can get greens now whenever we want them   we drawed some fish last Saturday which went off very wel   we get plenty to eat and that that is good enough   I am going to send henry a feather to put on his hat   it is one that I got with my hat   I dont care about wearing it so I wil send it to him   would like to send sis something but I hant got any thing now   I wil try and get something that I can send to her in a letter by the time I write again   I wil send you a few cotton seed so you can raise your own cotton if you want to   I rote to mother yesterday and sent her 75 or 80 seed   I got a letter from Richard the same time I got yours   tel him I wil answer it in a few days   tel the rest all to write   I would be glad to get a letter from any of them and wil gladly answer any letter that is wrote to me to the best of my ability   I want you to write often for I am always glad to hear from you   I wil quit for this time
this from your affectionate husband
Wm Coffin To Rachel L Coffin and the children

Camp Elliott   Corinth   Miss
April the 1st, 1863

Respected brother   it is with the greatest of pleasure that I embrace the present to write you a few lines in answer to your very exceptable letter which received a few days ago and read with the greatest of pleasure   I am happy to inform you that I am wel at present hopeing that when this comes to hand it wil find you enjoying the same great blessing   our boys are generally wel and in the best of spirits   we have had pretty cool weather for 3 day past   it frosted last knight and the knight before considerable   I think the fruit must all be killed in this part of the country   I wil give you the prices of a few articles at this place   butter is worth from 40 to 50 per lb eggs 40 per doz salt 10 per lb coffee 40 cts and other things in proportion   boots are worth from 6 to $50 a pair citizens are starving out and comeing in here for protection all the time the authorities here are sending them up to Tennese where they can make their own grub   it dont pay goverment to feed 2 or 3 thousand citizens that ant doing any thing for their country guarding rebel property and feeding rebel citizens is about plaid out   I wil conclude fore the present by requesting you to write when convenient   I wil write a little to Luzenah which you wil please tel her if you have the opportunity
yours truly
Wm Coffin

Dear wife   as I have bin writing some to Richard and have a little blank paper left I wil scratch you a line I rec yours of the 23 on the 28th which was a little quicker than letters generally come through   I got yours of the 17 & 19th and answered both of them I guess the most of your letters have come through   we wil be paid some in a few days   we signed our pay rolls yesterday   it is going to be very uncertain busines send it home but I shall risk it by send a little at a time in letters   I guess we wil get 5 months pay if we do I aim to send you $40   I want you to pay your father and mine to for what you have eat and the trouble you have bin   I want you to keep every thing strait for you know more about things there than I do   it costs them something to keep you and I want them to be paid so they wont loose any thing   I think I am able to keep you yet and I want to do it   when you buy flour buy the best there is   I have good flour and I want you to   I want you to live as wel as you can under the present circumstances   if Anderson dont send you any money I wil send more than $40 I am going to write to him to pay what I owe up there and not send any to you unless he has already don it   tel the children I got their candy and was very glad to get a present from them   would be glad to send them some presents but I dont know what I could get that I could send in a letter   I sent

henry a feather to put in his hat and I allow to send sis something as soon as I can get anything that I can send   I was going to send you some cotton seed in my last letter and forgot to put them in   I wil send a few in this and you can plant them if you want   if you dont you can give them to somebody else   write and tel me whether you have got so you can read my letters yet or not no more at present
yours truly
William Coffin

Sunday just after dinner
April the 5th 1863

Affectionate wife
 it is with pleasure that I once more take my pen for the purpose of addressing you a few lines   I am wel and I hope this wil find you and my dear little children well   we have beautiful weather here now   stil a little cool of knights it frosted some last knight   the boys are generally wel or getting wel Krysher is getting along very well   William Davenport is on the mend   I received your letter of the 24 & 25 a few days ago   your letter seem to have come through pretty strait lately   I answer all I get and very often write when I dont get any   Bill Louis one of our boys that was taken prisner got here last knight the rest wont be here probably for some time for ant exchanzed yet   I was at meeting this four noon   heard unkle Jonathan preach a very good sermon we have very good meetings down here but it looks a little lonesome to se no lovely women and dear little children there   we hope soon to have this rebelion put down and be permitted to return home to our familyes and friends   I think that when our army commences to moove in 3 months they wil find the rebels in a close corner   the roads are getting so that our forces can soon make a generel move and by that moove I think falls the southern confederacy which wil cause great rejoiceing north and south   as this is easter Sunday I suppose you wil have lots of eggs and other good things so I wil tel you what we had for breakfast and dinner   we had a good mess of fish and biscuit and coffee for breakfast and for dinner we had a rice pudding got up in the best of style crackers and meat   I dont know what we wil have for supper but something good no doubt we are liveing very wel now   I guess we wil draw some fish from this an we hant got our money yet but I guess we wil be paid off one day this week   I dont know certain how I wil undertake to send it to you   it is rather dangerous sending money   any way the express co wont be responsible if it is destroyed by the rebels   tel sis I hant got her any present yet but I wil get something and send to her as soon as I can   write to me whether henrys fether got through or not   I would like to send them lots of little presents but I dont have much chance to get any thing here   in fact I hant much to get with you wanted to know in one of your letters what I had done with the cow and

calf I sold them to Anderson last fall   I wrote to you then but I suppose you dident get the letter   I got $9 .for her and the calf I never wrote to you I believe how ignorant the people is down here people up north wil talk about the ignorance of the negro but they are just as smart as the poor white people there is lots of women comes to our picket line and want pases to go in to town to trade that cant tell what county they live in   that is no hear say   we witness it nearly every day when we are on picket they ask them where they live and they wil say in Missisipi   There was one old woman come to the lines said she used to live in Miss but she mooved six miles about a year ago and she dident know whether she lived in Miss now or not   I must conclude for this time write and tel me whether you have got so you can read my letters yet or not   I wil send you a percimon seed and a few more cotton seed maybe somebody would like to have them

with love and respect I remain yours truly

Wm Coffin to Luzenah

April the 13th 1863

Dear wife   It is with pleasure that I once more take my pen for the purpose of addressing you a few lines   I am wel as comon and hope this wil find you wel   I received the letter you and Lydia Ann & Nathan a few days ago   I would have rote sooner but was waiting to see if we would get any money   we got our green backs yesterday   we got pay up to the first of March which amounted to $74.50   I hant hardly come to a conclusion how much I wil send you   I have bin thinking some of paying Krysher some that I owe him   if I do I wil send you $40   if I dont pay him any on the land I wil send you $60 I have paid him $5   I owed him in a seperate note   it is such uncertain business sending it home that I hardly know what to do about it   I shall send some of it by express and some in letters   I wont send any in this   am going to send a receipt from Jim Carpenter which I want you to take care of & write to me as soon as you get it I want you to be very careful with all the papers you have in your care   Anderson writes that he has sent you five dollars   if you get it and $40 from me I think wil make you plenty til we are paid again   for is a special order that the soldiers are to be paid every 2 months from the first of last month I want to square up every thing I owe as quick as I can   I guess Anderson sold my corn and wheat for enough to pay my tax and what other debts I am owing up there   Isaac Mills writes that unkle Middleton got their old house burnt with all their meat molasses bed clothes and the most their wearing clothes   besides ruined about half their new house that they was building by the side of the old one   I am going to town this after noon and wil come to some conclusion about the money before I send this   have bin to town I tried get a nice little present to send to sis but I couldent find any thing that was suitable so I want you to by her one for me write and tel me whether hen-

rys fether come through safe or not   I have come to the conclusion to pay
krysher more so I wil send you $40   I want you to settle up with all you owe
and send me word how much money you have left after doing so   I want you
to keep things all strait so there wil be no trouble in your settlements with any
one you may have dealings with   I took a hot peach pie while I was in town
I wish you could have helped eat it for it was splendid   they only cost 20 cts
here   the most of things are pretty high   butter is worth 50 cts a pound   I
dont know of any thing more that would interest you & I wil conclude for this
time   Write soon and often for I am always anxious to hear from you   tel
all the news & C
this from your affectionate husband
Wm Coffin to R. L. Coffin & children

I will send $2.00 in this

April the 14th

Dear wife   I now seat myself to write you a line in answer to yours of the 8th
which I received last knight   it come through the quickest of any letter I have
had since I come here   I wrote you a letter yesterday   put in a recipt from
Jim Carpenter and $2.00 in money   I did aim to send half the money by let-
ter $2 at a time but we are ordered away from here   we have to start at day-
light tomorrow morning and I shal start the money by express this evening   I
wil send $40   I bought me a gum blanket today it cost me $5   they are a
great help when it rains person can lay out all night in the rain and get up dry
I have paid Krysher $25 20 on the land and 5 I owed him besides   I owe
him 20 yet which O C macy wil pay   which wil let me out of that trade which
I think has proved to be a good one   I dont know where we wil go to   we
are only ordered to take two days rations in our haversacks but probably there
wil be teams to haul provisions   I am going to send sis a little present in this
I dont know of any thing more to write at present   so I wil conclude write
soon tel me whether the money comes through safe or not
I remain yours truly
Wm Coffin to Rachel L Coffin

Corinth Miss
May the 3rd, 1863

Dear wife   as it has bin sometime since I have had an opportunity of writing I wil now try to write you a few lines giveing a description of our trip   we started from here the 15th of April went to Burnsville and camped   16th went to Iuka and took dinner   went on to clear creek and camped   17th all our regt and the trains which we war left to guard went on to bear creek where the rebs war said to be in considerable fore and in a strong position   our batteries war planted on a high hill on this side where they commenced shelling to woods on the other in order to find where the rebs war   fortunately about three of our first shell lit rite in their camp killing 3 and the rest skedadled   our cavalry followed them some 5 or 6 miles and had some sharp skirmishing in the evening   we mooved up with the train   18th our cavalry some infantry and some artilery followed the rebs   had some sharp skirmishers   some killed on both sides   we lost 2 pieces of artillery and about 40 men taken prisner   19 got our guns back & severel prisners   war reinforced by another brigade in the evening which fetched our mail to us   I got a letter from you that you rote the day you left fathers   one from dick rote the 12th and one from thol and Abigail   20th more soldiers coming fetched us more mail   I got a letter from you rote I believe the 13th and one from father and mothere   all quiet 22   all quiet 23   marched on crossed buzzard roost cane creeks & C and camped in the woods by a large farm which afforded plenty of rails for fire   24 went on to stinking bear creek where the rebs war said to be fortified   got there found a few rails piled up for them to hide behind but none of them there went on to tuscumbia expecting a big fight there certain but in stid of fighting they run as though their shirt tails war afire, camped all round town   our cavalry followed the rebs and took in 80 of them Tuscumbia is a nice place   two springs there that make a creek large enough to run a mile   25 laid at tuscumbia   26 stil at tuscumbia   Call hil cowger D C harper and myself on picket killed a fat pig that would weigh 60 net   made a big fire out of rails and rosted all of it it was nice enough for any bodys wedding dinner   27th went on 12 miles to old town creek where there was some skirmishing and they throwed severel shel over at us but done no harm   the rebs on one side and us on the other the bridge burnt and the creek swimming   28th they commenced shelling us as soon as it was light   we got our breakfast as though there wasent a reb in 100 miles   about 6 oclock our batteries commenced firing first one and then another til I guess they all got the range on them and then they let loose from 5 different points all at the same time which made them soon scratch gravel   they now took a position about 2 miles from us   the first was a mile and a half they only had one gun that would reach us from this place   we had severel that would reach them   it was a nice thing to look at   we could see our shel burst around them and see the smoke from their gun   both forces war on an open field   a lot of us was on a high point looking at them and they commenced on us   the first shel they throwed lit close enough to throw dirt in some of our boys eyes   we could se them comeing in time to dodge them they war so near spent by the time they got to where we that we could run out of of the way they have a whiz that I dont like the sound of   they cant be seen when it is clear   about 10 oclock our men commenced making a bridge to cross over on   the rebs tried very hard to shell them back from the crek but all in vain   they wounded 3 of our men slightly was all the damage was done to our forces all day   about 1 oclock the shelling ceased and the 1st brigade crossed over on the railroad bridge which they had bin afraid to do before for fear of the rebs haveing guns that would rake the road   about 3 they got the other bridge fixed so our brigade crossed   there was skirmishers throwed out and we advanced in line of battle for a mile   the skirmishers got a few shots at them a good way of   as they run we commenced killing hogs and chickens for supper   when we war ordered back to where we camped the nite before got back a little after dark found our quartermaster with 50 head of sheep ready butchered for us cooked our supper   roasted a sheep leg apiece for next day and went to bed   29th started back   burnt the railroad bridge which I think was the main thing we come for   I wil just say we had the first Alabama cavalry with us which war to a great extent made up rite in this part of Ala   when they left for to keep from being presed in to the rebel service the rebs burnt their houses and took their property   of all times and now they thought was their time   although very contrary to generel Dodge orders before daylight old town as it is called was in flames   it is to big planters lives close to gether they had had so many negroes that their shantys made it look like town from that on we could se houses burning all the time no difference which way we looked we got to tuscumbia about noon   dont think there was a dozen houses in five miles of the road on either side but what was burnt   went on to stinking bear creek and camped   I forgot to say that the citizens had all fled to the mountains with their mules horses negroes bacon & C   all that staid at home saved their houses and all that left got them burnt   they dident burn any houses where the people was at home   this valey clear from big bear to old town is very good country   better than I ever expected to find in dixey   all owned by rich men   about 5 acres out of 100 in cultivation and at present it is a poor prospect of them making much off of what they have in in   they plant corn all together   30th started found the road side perfectly lined with darky that had corne in through the night to go to Corinth   they most all had a bundle of old duds   10 oclock got your letter with the candy   carrying some had enough to load a mule went on to buzard creek   took dinner and put up for the nite   wating for them to get a flat boat or rather a raft fixed to take us over here   the quartermaster got 50 head of sheep for us   we killed all and what we dident want then we salted an hauled along   against I got my leg roasted and got in bed it was ten oclock   at eleven we war called up to cross the creek

we war the first that crossed   it took til 10 next day to get all the force across
May 1st went on to Burnsville & camped   2 got all that was sick or had sore
feet on the cars and the rest of us footed it we got here about an hour by sun
when we got here we found that there was $30,000 worth of cotton about 1,000
negroes and no telling how many horses and mules had followed us in to take
care of them as they are in our lines   tel the copperheads if you se any that
if they want to do any thing for their friends in the south that they had better do
some thing for their friend in tuscumbia valley for they have no head to stick
their holes in   we lived as wel as men could live   I expect we killed a mil-
lion of hogs 5,000 cattle all the chickens geese & C that we could manage cut-
ting the thing short we cleaned the whole valley out of every thing that we
could use   it had bin a great for the rebel cavalry to get subsistence but I guess
they wil get out with empty guts next time we mooved in all the union folks
that wanted protection   I stood the trip wel   never felt better in my life for
the same length of time I stand marching as wel as any man in the company
Weir & Krysher Mack Coons and severel others wasent out   the boys that
was sick are all better   most of them getting stout W F Davenport has got his
discharge and gone home   I got your letter last knight of the 26th stating that
you had got the money which I was glad to hear   we got mail while we was
out every few days but had no chance to send any but once and that day I was
on picket and dident know there was a chance til it was to late   we war clean
of of any mail route at all   you can do as you think best about keeping house
I want you to by plenty of flour and other things that you need to eat and wear
I dont want you nor the children to live on any thing you dont like   I think I
can send you money enough to keep you in plenty of every thing   I must quit
tel Dick I wil write to him in a few days   I dont feel much like writing today
I slept to hard last knight for we hadent got to sleep much for 2 nites
before   I dont expect you can read what I have rote
this from your affectionate husband
Wm Coffin to R L C

Oliver & I got a letter from Anderson while we was gone   they war al wel
John Y. Davenport is married to Cas Hickenbottom   I reckon he wil make that
spyglass of his sit up and brindle   they are two heavy purps   if a boddy
dident care what they said I expect they wil get rich this Summer   old Ab is
going to the peak this spring with all his family and Wil henry to bad I hope
they wil never get back   I hope old ab wit have to fight Indians all the way so
that he wil know how soldiering goes Anderson says Caldwel raised 9 lambs
out of 3 he dident write how the sheep was doing   if you have yarn to spare
I wish you would knit and send me a pair of socks we can get plenty here but
they dont last long and they are sowed up at the tow which makes a seam that
hurts a persons toes on a march   they do wel enough about camp   I dont
want a very heavy pair   if you send them send them by mail   put them up

in a piece of paper and direct it as you would a letter the postage wont be much some of the boys have got them by mail for 5 cts other cost 20 cts   I would like to se you and the children very wel but I want the rebs all whiped first which I hope wont be long   a few more such rades as we made wil bring them to their milk and I understand there was an expedition on each side of us at the same time doing the same kind of work   no more this time yours as ever Wm C to R L C

Sunday morning May the 10th 1863

Dear wife   I now take my pen to write you a line though I dont know that I have any thing of interest to communicate only that I am wel   the boys are generaely getting stout and in fine ability   the war news seem to be more cheering for a few days than common   if Hooker comes out right at Richmond I think the war wil close soon which of course we would all be glad of   we have had very nice weather for some time   not as warm as I expect- ed it would be from the way the spring commenced   every thing is growing fine   garden stuff is getting large enough to use   corn where there is any is large enough to plow and other things in proportion   I hant had a letter from you for a week   I got one from father & mother and one from Jim and Phebe and one from I J Mills Tuesday night they war all wel   Isaac is a heavy prurp he expresses himself pretty freely   I have bin writing a long letter to him today I expect I wil get fits next time he rites if he rites at all there is a chance to get furlows now   five out of every hundred can get furlows for 20 days   but sick men have the preference so there ant much chance for me to get one while I keep my health as I have had it and I hope I may   I would be very glad to se you and the children but if I could get a furlow   20 day would only give time to go there and back   I want you to take care of yourself and the children by plenty of every thing you want to eat get the best there is going   dont feed the children on corn bread   I think I am able to furnish the little things something that they can eat yet a while   I want you to enjoy yourself the best you can til I get home, I get along very wel considering the circumtances, I hant heard any thing particular about the sheep yet   I rote to old Johny last week I shall look for a letter from him soon   anderson rote that he had raised 9 lambs   I want you to write what you want done with the wool   I expect the wool wil sel for a fair price   I rote to old John that I would let him have wool for his lamb if he would set it   dine wil have a colt this season   tel sis it wil be hers as george died   she must have a little horse   I dont know of any thing more at present so I wil conclude   write soon and often and tel all the news and tel the rest to write   I would be glad to get a letter from any of them
yours affectionately
Wm Coffin to all

Corinth Miss
May the 15th, 63

Dear wife   I again take my pen for the purpose of writing you a few lines though I hant any thing of importance to write   only that I am wel and hope this wil find you and the children wel   I hant had a letter from you for nearly two weeks which makes me feel uneasy about you   the last I got was the one you rote in answer to the one I rote the day before we started on that trip I should have rote sooner but stil expected from day to day to get a letter from you   besides I had no news to write   dont want you to quit writing because we are ordered away from here   for we wil get the letters some time and I shall write to you often when I am where I can   It is altogether likely that we wil take another trip in a week or so   if we do we wil be likely to get where there is no regular mail   we had generel review yesterday and severel good speeches   one from Adjutant Generel Thomas of united states Army   he was our reviewing officer   he is rite from Washington City   sent by the President to assist in organizing and fitting up regiments of negroes for the service   we have got our houses all done and in them about 75 in all in our regiment   we are fixed very comfortable   our houses are better than lots of houses in Iowa that people winter in   we hant had any very hot weather yet   it is cool of nites all the time, and but few days warmer than comon for this time of year in Iowa   Wm Mcmullen got a discharge and started home yesterday morning he hant ever bin able for duty since we left Iowa   Jim Mitchel is stil sick   the rest of our company are doing wel   I guess Jim wil get a furlow and go home in a few days   there is a chance for 3 at a time to get furlows from our co Mat Noel Charley graham & Jim wil go first   I dont know of any thing more to write at present and I have to go on picket at 7 oclock so I wil quit and get ready   write soon and often   tel me all the news & C   I had no news from Dallas lately
yours affectionately
Wm Coffin to Rachel L Coffin & children

Sunday morning May the 24th 1863

Dear wife   I take the present to answer your very exceptable letter of the 15 & 16 which I received last knight and read with much pleasure for I hadent had a letter from you for 4 week which made me very anxious to hear from you   I am wel at present   the health of the camp is generally pretty good   we have nice wether   no rain for a month   the dust is getting pretty deep which would make it very disagreeable if we war to have to march but I dont hear of any prospect of us haveing to go out again soon   I rote to father that I wanted him to make.his charge and I want you to pay him and I want you to pay your father I want every thing paid up so I wil no what kind of circumstances I am in and what to depend on I want if ever get home to be out of debt   tel them they had better take pay while they can get it for maybe they wont have a chance again soon   tel Henry I would like to se his pet squirrels for they are such nice things for pets   would like to se their little toe heads jumping around playing with their squirrels for I know they have big times   I aim to try to get a furlow this fall if I can and I think I can if any body can   they are only giveing furlows for 20 days now I hate to go on a 20 day furlow for I would only have time to go there and back   I think after the main fighting season is over they wil give furlows for 30 days   I aim to se you this fall if I can   I dont want to go north while it is hot weather for fear of it makeing me sick when I come back   I want you to get along the best you can   keep plenty of every thing to eat and wear   I want you to live as wel as you can and not try to lay up money   if I ever get home I think I can make a liveing if we dont have much to start with   I have to go on picket and cant finish this til tomorow   this the 25th and I wil finish my letter   all wel this morning wether stil dry   we seen one reb yesterday while on picket but dident get a shot at him   I have had no news from dallas lately   I want you to write what you want done with the wool   whether you want it sold or not   Jess Williams come down last Friday night and stayed with me til Saturday in the afternoon   I am going up there next Saturday morning and stay til Sunday evening   I am going to get 15 or 20 lbs of butter   some eggs onions & C they are plenty up there and cheaper than they are here   you needent to mind sending any down unless you just want want to send it as a present   it wont cost me much more here than it wil cost to send it from up there here it was reported here last knight that generel dodge got a telegrap dispatch from old Rosencrantz   I hope it is so   I suppose you wil hear it if it is so before you get this,   I dont know any about the money matter yet   I hope to get a letter from Anderson soon giveing some satisfaction about things up there   I am going to send the children some peach blossoms as you may not have a chance to se any in Iowa   they have bin in bloom about 2 weeks here   it is raining considerable to day   I dont know of any thing more that would interest you so I wil quit

with love I remain your affectionate husband

Wm Coffin To Rachel L Coffin

a line to Benny Moris   wel Benny I would like to be where I could have a chat with you today as it is raining and I have nothing else to do   we are getting along fine down here now   we ant doing any of fighting but we are ready to give the rebels fits whenever we have a chance   I guess we wil be kept here for a while to guard Corinth   I guess they wil never attack this place again   if they do it wil be bad for them unless they have a powerful force for

we are wel fortified   I hope we wil get the rebels on the run before long   I feel in hopes that before hot weather comes we wil have them to the jumping off place and ready to make a bayonet charge on them   I must quit for this time   write me a letter if you feel like it and I wil do better next time this your friend as ever
Wm Coffin

friday evening May the 29th 1863

Dear wife
I take the present to inform you that I am wel at present and hope those few lines wil find you and the children wel   I received the socks you sent last night they are just the kind I wanted   I hope to be able to do as much for you some-time   health is about like it was when I rote last   Olivcr is complaining today but nothing serious their   Couch has a felon on his finger which is hurting him some   not to its worst yet   we have had some very warm weather lately   we drill a half hour every morning and three quarters in the evening skirmish with the graybacks and wood ticks   the ballance of the time we live wel and have as good times as soldiers could expect to have   O. C. Macy and I have divided blankets   the noncommissioned officers have to all live in one house   Oliver being a sergeant he had to go in with them   he is a good fellow for a partner   I aim to go up to the 16 mile watter tank in the morning to se Jess Williams   go a fishing   get some eggs butter onions & C if I can get a pass   we got good news from Vicksburg last night which I hope wil prove true   our negro soldiers are learning to drill very fast   they turn their whole attention to it   they are keen to get to try the rebs a hitch they have great confidence in their selves   I dont know how they wil do but I believe they wil do good fighting   I sent you a paper a few days ago   there is some prospect of us haveing to do post duty here   I dont like the idea much though it wil exempt us from going on marches & C   if we get the position our work wil be guarding the stockade where the prisners are kept   the generels head quarters   the post comisary & C & C   I would rather do picket duty Weir got a letter from Dallas stating that Anderson had started to Jefferson suppose they are gone back before this time   I dont get any news from old Johny yet about our wool   I want you to write what you want done with it   I dont know of any thing more
this from your affectionate husband and friend as ever
Wm Coffin To Rachel L Coffin

Corinth Miss
May the 31 st 1863

Affectionate wife   I now seat myself for the purpose of writing you a few lines
in answer to your kind letter ofthe 21st which found me wel   I was sorrow
to hear of sis being sick   I hope she wil be better before you get this   I want
you to tel me how she is getting along in your next letter   I want you to have
her doctored when you think she needs it and take as good care of her and henry
& yourself as you can   if sis gets mueh very sick I want you to write and I
wil try to get a furlow and come home dont want a furlow til fall if you keep
wel   if I get one now it wil be nearly 2 years before I could get another if the
war lasts that long   I would like to see henry todling off to school   I expect
he makes quite a show   you wanted to know what I think of the war when
it wil over & C   I give much idea the rebels are whiped to death now, but they
may keep fighting and retreating for a year yet   I dont think they can last more
than 15 months at the outsid if our forces push forward as they have done they
wont fight us now unles they have 5 to our one or have fortifications to fight
behind the socks came through one day sooner than the letter which I suppose
you sent at the same time   I am wel. pleased with the socks they are just the
kind I wanted   I wil send you a present as soon as I have a chance to get one
that I can send in a letter   it ant because I dont think about you that I hant
sent one before but because it is hard to get any thing   wel I was on picket yesterday our company holds the outpost on the hamburg road we stay a quarter
further out than the main picket line so we get to se all the citizens that comes
in on that road and we stop them there til we send in to the next post where the
officers of the guard stays to get orders whether to let them in or not   we have
good chance to buy all kinds of vegetables milk butter & C   we have 6 on the
post at a time yesterday.   we bought a quart of strawberys mulberrys apiece
and a quart of buttermilk apiece for dinner   each cost us 10 cts a quart   we
had our mulberries stewed and sugar in them and we had good lite bread and
ham meat so you had better think we had a good diner   I wish you could have
had some   I know you would have said it was bully, but the trouble was before
morning   the boys all but me had the Mississipi quickstep so that it kept them
running two at a time   I aim to buy enough butter and eggs when I go up to
Bethel so that I can sell enough to get my money back and have enough left for
my own use   butter is worth 25 cts up there & 50 here eggs 20 up there 40
down here so you se I can make something on it   it dont cost any thing to go
up there on the cars they are camped on cipress creek and they have a fish sane
and we are going a fishing Jess says they have all the fish they want   we
wont be likely to get any pay again til the 1st of July when we wil be likely to
get 4 months pay   you wouldent know Krysher if you was to se him   he
looks old as his daddy and as fat as a bear his hair has nearly all come out   he
has had the sore eyes for some time pretty bad   the boys are generally a heap

fatter than they war in Iowa   I am lighter than I was when I left Davenport but I am in good health as I ever was   I dont know of any thing more so I wil bring my letter to a close write often without fail
yours with respect
Wm Coffin

Tuesday   June the 2nd   1863

Dear wife   As I have a little leisure this evening   I wil write you a few lines though I have nothing of importance to write I am wel as comon and do hope this wil find you and the children wel   we hade a nice rain this morning which was needed very bad to lay the dust & C   O. C. Macy hant bin wel for a few days he hant went to the hospital yet and I hope he wont have to   I am the only man in our company but what has bin sick more or less   I have never reported sick to the doctors yet   I have had no news from Dallas lately   I wish you could be here to eat with me as I am cooking for one mess this week we are fareing the best lately we eaver have   we have ham meat altogether and the best of bread   we have regimental baker and he makes splendid bread we have mor coffee tea and sugar than we can use   we have a barrel of rice ahead   we got all the potatoes & beans we want   we sell enough coffee to buy what little extras we want for the mess   I wish you had some of our coffee sugar & rice   I want you to buy all such things you want   get some dried fruit for I know you are fond of it   when I want any I buy it and I want you to live as wel as I do   I am going to send you a soldiers song book it is old and dirty but the songs are good
as ever yours truly
W C

(Note: June 2, 63   Separate page   No date)

in the evening there was 7 rebel hogs come along   the first I have seen close here since we come here   they wouldent take the oath so we fired in to them killing 4 and the rest retreated in disorder   I shot 3 at 2 shots that is doing pretty wel   we sold enough to pay for our mulberrys and buttermilk and had all the pork left that the whole company wanted   our negro regiment drawed their new clothes yesterday   they war mached down to a little creek close to our picket post and there they all striped off   took a good wash and put on their uniform which made them look quite soldier like   they are awful anxious to get a dig at the rebs   since I have bin writing Generel Carmine came with his Cavalry   they have bin out 6 days had 2 or three little brushes with the rebs   they fetched in about 100 prisners   severel officers   any amount of

horses mules and negroes and one rebel flag   couldent get a pass to go up the
railroad   I think I wil get one in a few days   I am cook this week   I com-
mence today   I dread it while it stays warm   we dont bake our own bread
now which makes it easyer on the cooks   we draw hams lately alltogether
which suits us exactly   you said you hadent had a letter for a good while   I
have rote once a week and oftener the most of the time   Jim Mitchel wil be sent
north to some generel hospital in a few days probably to Keokuk   he is pretty low   he is stil able to walk round but he looks like a skeleton   there wil
be 25 from the regt sent away   I dont know of any thing more to write this
time so wil quit   write soon give my best respects to all good union men   tel
the copperheads if you se any they had better be on their knees begging for
mercy than to be gassing around and insulting loyal women and children   the
time wil come I hope when the soldiers wil get to go home and then to my opinion copperheads wil be the most comon fruit you wil se on the trees in Iowa
the soldiers love a rebel in arms to what they do a copperhead   it make me
so mad sometimes when I hear what they do that I just want to get to kill some
of them   I wil quit for this time   write often
this from your affectionate husband
Wm Coffin To R. L Coffin and children

Note: Approximate Date is June 9, 1863

Dear wife   as I have bin writing some to Jim and Phebe I wil try to write
some to you   I received your letter of the tenth and was glad to hear that you
and the children was wel   I guess you wil get letters more regular than you
have   they have the railroad fixed now between Jackson & Columbus   I
have rote once a week and some times oftener   I hant forgot you yet nor never
wil while I live   you and the children are the most dear to me of any thing in
this world but you know I cant come home to you now and I want you to make
yourself as wel contented as posible   you to know what I think about you
keeping house   it mite do well enough in the summer time if you could get
a house close to fathers or your fathers   dont think it would be best for you to
go home as it is to far from where anybody lives and you know you ant able to
zo through the hardships you would have to undergo   if you could get a house
handy and live in it in the summer and when cold weather come you could
moove in with some of them   I think it would be better than for you to move
home   I dont want you to expose your self more than you cant help for and I
dont believe you would be satisfied if you was at home   you must make yourself as wel contented as posible til I get home   I am going to take every thing
as easy as posible for it dont do any good to fret about anything about money
I guess we wil get some the last of this month if we are paid now soon we wil
get $52 dollars   I wil send you some as soon as I get any   I owe Jim

Carpenter 4.50 yet I want to pay and I want to keep enough so I can have some to by little extras to eat when ever I feel like I wanted something and the rest I wil send to you   I wil send you 30 or 35 dollars and you can use it as you please but I dont se how you can get things enough to keep house with unless you could get an old stove and bedsteads & C   you can use your own pleasure about where you stay   I want you to enjoy yourself the best you can and as you have to take care of your self you can bet better than I can what wil suit you I expect to send you all the money I can spare all the time only what it wil take to pay what little I am owing and if   I dont draw any before long I wil have dines sold if you need money   I dont expect for you to suffer for any thing that I can help   tel Williamses folks Jess was over to see me today and we had a good talk about all our friends at home   Jess is getting stout and hearty   he says he got a letter from Johnathan 3 or 4 week ago he was near Memphis   then he hant had any word from Newton lately   I am glad that it is so that we can get to see one another once in a while for I always thought as much of Jess as any fellow I ever was acquainted with   it is bed time and I must quit   write soon and often and keep me posted about how you are getting along and all about the children & C   tel father and mother I wit write to them soon
this from your affectionate husband
Wm Coffin To R L Coffin

William Tawney and Jesse Rosencranz left here last saturday and hant bin seen since by us   they are either gone home or have bin taken prisner

June the 14th 63
Sunday Morning

Dear wife   I take the present opportunity to write you a few lines in answer to your letter dating from May 31st to June the 6th which I received last evening   I was glad to hear from you and to hear that you and the children war wel th is leaves me about as comon. I have had a kind of rheumatisom in my hip for a few days past which was rather disgreeable though not so but what I could go   it is about wel now   there is nothing going on here more than comon   the guerrillas have bin around lately more than comon   they have picket up   a few of our men that war out gathering berrys & C   lately they have taken 2 to 5 of our men lately they had got in a way of going out 2 or 3 miles for berrys and apples cherrys & C   the gurrillas never ventured so close here before since we have bin here   tel henry he must be a good boy when he goes to school and learn as fast as he can so he can rite pop letters   tel sis she must let her mother learn her til she gets biger   tel them I want them to keep their pet squirrels if they can til I get home and I wil get them a cage to put them in   I hant had a letter from dallas for a good while   I dident know Andersons was going to Jefferson in time or I would have rote for them to take the wool   I rote to old Johny to keep the wool not knowing that there would be any chance to sent it to you   he hant never rote to me whether they want the wool or not   you had better buy what wool you want for I know that I can sel that,   you had better keep what silver you have for it wil be very scarce before long   we dont ever se any here atal   I guess we wil draw for furlows for this on so it wil be very uncertain when a fellow wil get one   this fall and maybe I wont get one for 2 years   it is just owing to what kind of luck I have a drawing   you must take things easy and to providence to fetch things all right they have matched   Jess Rosencrats one of the men that deserted from our co they have sent a petition to Cap Marsh requesting him to do all he can to make his sentence as light as posible   I dont hardly think they wil shoot him   they catched him out in Nebraska   he is at Davenport now hope he wil never be permited to come to the company   dont want such a man in the co.   I am going to send you and the children some raisons in this as long as I cant be with you I wil send you a Sunday morning present   Sunday is the lonesomist day we have here   I dont know of any thing more so I wil quit for now

from your affectionate husband

Wm Coffin To Rachel L Coffin and little ones

June the 16th 1863

Dear wife   I take my pen to write you a few lines in answer to yours of the 9th which I received this morning   I was glad to hear that you was all wel   I am tolerable wel but dont feel quite as stout as comon,   you made quite a mistake in reading my letter or I made a mistake in writing about killing any body I dont recollect just what I did write but I guess I rote that we killed 4 rebel hogs at any rate that is what we done there ant much difference between rebels and hogs and if there was a gang of rebs to come we would try to use them like we did the hogs   I was glad to hear that sis had got stout again   I hope you all continue to be blessed with good health   health here is about as comon   O. C. Macy has bin sick for some time but not serious   he is getting up and about again   Weir is as stout as he ever was in his life krysher ant rite stout yet but he is so fat that he cant hardly waddle he got a letter the other evening stating that his mother was laying not expected to live   I hant had a letter from Dallas lately   I dont know of any thing more that would interest you so I wil quit take good care of your self and children

your as ever Wm Coffin

44

June the 18th 63

Dear wife

I this morning take my pen to drop you a line in answer to yours of the 12th which I received last evening and red with pleasure   I am just tolerable wel wel I have bin rather funy for a few days past but stil able to be up and about I feel better this morning think I wil be all right in a day or to   we got a letter amongst us last evening from Anderson   they war wel   nothing strange going on up there   I hant got a letter from Caldwel yet   I expect I can sell the wool to them but I dont know but it would be better to get them to work it up on the shares I shant be in any hurry to dispose of it in any way   there is nothing of any interest going on here now   Tom vancleave was converted last week   he is as strong a union man as we have now now he got to examineing the scriptures to proove himself right and by so doing got convinced that he was rong   he frankly acknowledged the error of his ways and now he seems like a new man   our our company are all on one side now which I think is the right side   I dont know of any thing more to write this time so I wil conclude this

from your affectionate husband

Wm Coffin To R L Coffin & C

Corinth Miss June the 28th

Dear wife   I take my pen to write you a few lines in answer to your letter of the 19 which I received 2 days ago and dident answer it rite away because I had just rote you one the day before I am about wel of the janders   I am able for duty now but I dont intend to go on duty til I get pretty stout   we have had a goodel of rain here lately   I think corn wil be good down here this season though I hant bin out to se any crops we any amount of blackberys here   we make all the pies we want   some of the boys can make as good pies as any woman   I hant tried it yet   we have plenty of everything to eat except garden stuff and milk and butter   garden stuff is dear and scarce   onions is worth 25 cts a dozen and not large at that   we can get all the butter we want at 40 cts a lb O C Macy got 50 lbs from home a day or two ago   it was nice butter it cost about 30 cts a lb by the time he got it here   I got enough to do me a week or so   tel henry and sis they must be very careful with their squirrels as they wil run off   if they keep them til I get home I wil get them a cage to put them in cant tel you any thing about when I wil get to come home I aim to get a furlow this fall if I can but it a little uncertain   I want you to tel me how you are fixed for keeping house   how your are getting along & C we heard a few days ago that jim Mitchel was dead   he left here 2 or 3 weeks ago for some post hospital   I dont recollect the place where he died   health here is about as comon   some of the letters you send are very poorly backed it is almost a I wonder that some of them come through at all   I wil send you an envelope directed right and you can keep it to direct by   it is very necessary to put the company number of the regiment and the state is from in plain so it cant be mistaken for some other regiment I wil coppy a few lines from the state register headed "Couldent have it - the copperheads who have control of a church building 8 miles east of winterset refused the use of their church on the occasion of the funerel Aaron Hollinback a soldier who died at Corinth Mrs Hollinback was informcd by the copperheads that she could not have the church for any such purpose" Hollinback was a member of co F in our regiment,   if that ant mean then the old boy wants them to be it   ant any use in talking about people being worse than he wants them to be.   this ant only a newspaper report but it is confirmed by letters to our boys from that part of the country   no more at this time

I sign myself as ever your husband and friend

W C to R L C

I wil send you a little present to keep your kneedle in

Corinth Miss July the 3rd 1863

Dear wife   I now take my pen to write you a few lines   I am wel at present and hope when this reaches you it wil find you and the children wel   I have got shed of the janders and feel as wel as comon   we have had very warm weather here for near a week past but not as hot as I have seen at this season in Iowa there ant a day passes but what I think of our brave boys that are laying in the ditches in the hot sun around vickburg &   their victory wil be complete and doubly pay them for all their hard ships   I guess the rebs are haveing a harder time than our boys which is some satisfaction to our boys no doubt   wel Luzenah we have blackberry pies or a cobler every day   I wish you could take a diner with us   all we lak to make our pies & coblers as good as any body can have is a little cream to make dip   we have sugar plenty we drawed beef pork and fish this last week so we have about any thing we want, there was 60 alabamians come in yesterday to enlist   they war all a horse back they said there was 40 more where they come from that wanted to get in but had no horses to ride they come about 60 miles   deserters stil come in every few days and give themselves up   say they wont fight any longer   they are begining to se how things are going   I hant had a letter from you for 5 or 6 days   I expect there wil be a big time here tomorrow as it is the 4th   I think we wil hear of grant giveing the rebs an interesting time tomorrow   I got a letter last evening from old Johny Moores folks   Bill is discharged and at home   Ike is married to nance Millys sister Micy as they called her   I

wont write any more til the mail comes as if I wont get a letter   3 oclock the mail come   I got your letter wrote the 24 and 27   I was glad to hear that you was wel   I would be very glad to be there and se you and the children once more   I dont know when I wil get a furlow   I want to get one this fall if I can   they ant giveing any furlows now nor wont be any more give til after the strugle at vicksburg is decided   you must take things easy as you can and wait with patience   I want to se you very bad but I know I cant be there all the time so I take things as calm as posible   you said you had got a paper that I sent you   I sent you two   I am going to send you a song ballad that has the right kind of doctrine in it   tel the children they must keep their pet squirrels wherever they go   I dont know any thing more to write this time so I wil quite
I remain your affectionate husband and friend as ever
Wm Coffin To Rachel L Coffin

Note: No Date
Probably July 4 or 5, 1863

Dear wife   I wil write you a line   I rote to you a day or to ago   also to father in the same letter   I hant had any letter from Dallas lately   I am looking for one from anderson all the time they are going to send Col Marshal home   they sent to Memphis today for a metalick coffin   the way he was murdered has raised the ambition of the boys generally and to my opinion the citizens had better not come around the picket line as they have bin doing or some of them wil come up missing   this thing of murdering our men in cold blood wont do   I wil send you that song ballad in this   I forgot to put it in the other letter   it is about time for the mail to go out and I hant any thing to write at best so I wil quit for this time   write when you can   I am always glad to get letter
I remain your affectionate husband and friend as ever
Wm Coffin To R. L. Coffin & children

Tuesday evening
July the 7th   1863

Dear wife   I now take my pen to write you a few lines in answer to yours of the 1st which I have just red   I am wel as comon and I hope when this reaches you it wil find you and the children wel tel them copperheads when their are calling us all thieves that we are proud of the name in the place of being called copperheads   we are working to put down the rebelion and if taking their property wil weaken them I say go in on it   I have never done any thing yet

that I am ashamed of   I have took in a few hogs and sheep and once in a while a chicken and I wouldent think I was a loyal man if I dident do all I could to starve them out   it is a little cooler today than it has bin for a few days   there was 2 of the kanses 7th shot yesterday while gathering berries about 2 miles from camp and this morning just at daylight   Co H was atacted where they war stationed 3 miles east of here guarding the mule carell   there was about 550 of the rebs and they had them completely surrounded before they new they war there   the pickets fired at them but they dashed in and the pickets was so close to camp that it dident hardly give our boys time to get their clothes on til the rebs war rite amongst them   stil the company formed in lines and give them a round or to   when the rebs surrounded them and war closeing in on them Cap Loomes told his boys to take care of themselves the best they could that it was imposible from to get out of there all together   some run 2 mile across an open field and made their escape but 27 men and the capt surendered the capt had his wife with him and they war staying in a house close by   he put on his soldier pants a bloush coat and an old white hat and took a gun instead of his sword to fight with so it is hoped he wil be paroaled as a private as he had nothing on to show that he is an officer   he is a splended captain and spunk to the back bone but he had no chance to fight   he was so completely surprised the rebs took all the mules out of the carell which amounted to 3 or 4 hundred but they war rundown mule put there to be recruited up our boys killed one lieutenant and one private and wounded one lieutenant and 3 privates   they had one man wounded pretty severe in the calf of his leg   we dont know how many wounded they carried away   2 of their wounded war found 2 miles from camp   all the cavalry force that was here war after them in an hour after they left   mules have bin comeing back all day which signifies that our men are crowding them   probably we wil hear something about how they come out by morning and I wil write it then Clark Bringham was taken is all the one that you was acquainted   I guess there was one of swallows boys taken   I dont know much about the furlow business   it is reported that Vicksburg is taken and I recon they wil give furlows again   our Capt has a very polite request to resign his office   he has 30 days to fix up things in and I dont expect we wil get much favors while he has command   we are going to give him a chance to resign and if he dont do it we wil find some other way to get him out   we dont like him any to wel at best but the trouble is he has bin drunk severel times in the last 3 weeks   the 4th he was so drunk he couldent navigate   we dont propose to patronize such conduct at the companys expense   if we should ever get in to an engagement with the rebs and him drunk it might be a dear thing to us   Price wil take his place Capt never drunk any of any consequence til lately   tel granny I would like to se her very wel tel her I would like to send her a present but I dont know of any thing that I could get that could be sent in a letter   wil quit for this time and write some to father and mother
I remain your husband as ever

Wm Coffin

wel father I dont know hardly what to write as it is so lately that I did write they fired a salute to day at 12 oclock over the surrender of Vicksburg they fired 16 guns it stil rains every few days which wil certainly make prety good crops down here unkle Jonathan is likely to get the position of regimental chaplain Jess Williams was over today he is wel I dont know of any thing to write so I wil quite for this time
this from they affectionate son
Wm Coffin

wel mother I wil try to write a line to thee though there is nothing that knows of to write that would interest the the wanted to know how we made out for something to eat I can say we have plenty we get fresh beef salt beef pork bacon and irish coffee tea sugar and rice dried fruit and potatoes and some molasses not much but we get all the sugar we want we get flour and crackers we get our flour baked at the the bakery we get very good bread our company sold 5 barrel of flour today and one of rice and we have 2 barrel of flour left so thee can se we have plenty what we sold come to $49 which wil be spent for what the company agree on we got a case of mackerel with some of it

Corinth Miss
July the 22 nd 1863

Dear wife I take my seat to write you a few lines in answer to your letter of the 15th which I was glad to get and to hear that you was all wel I am wel as comon and I hope when this comes to hand it wil find you and the children wel. times are about as comon here nothing of importance going on here there is a few prisners fetched in nearly every day the news seem to be so good lately that it looks like the rebels would play out pretty soon it is tolerable warm here now you wanted to know if there was any good looking women down here they are very scarce what there is are generally pretty hard looking pieces I hant seen any that was any temptation to me yet I have never broke any promises I made to you yet nor dont aim to if I stay down her my 3 years out I come here to fight for my country and not to disgrace myself and family I hope you have more confidence in me than to think I would have any thing to do with any other woman I dont know of any thing more to write this time
I remain you affectionate husband as ever
Wm Coffin To Rachel L Coffin

Dear sister   I now take my pen to scratch you a few lines in answer to your kind letter which I received a day or two ago   I dont know as I have any thing of importance to write   I am glad to hear that a copperhead gets justice once in awhile up there. I think if the soldiers cleans out the Southern rebels that the union men at home ought to clean out the northern rebels   stil if we get a chance we would be very glad to help clean out some of the copperheads   I think if our forces has as good luck for the next 12 months as they have had for the last 2 months there wont be much of the Southern Confederacy but what wil be demolished   I was over at the 7th yesterday   I dident se Jess he was on picket   I seen Sam goodwin   he is wel and said Jess was   he said Jess hadent had any word from the boys for some time,   wel Milton I would like to write some to you but I dont know any thing to write   hope you wil never let a chance slip to straiten a copperhead   make them afraid to show themselves in civil society wil quit for this time hopeing you wil excuse my poor letter write when convenient I wil try to answer a letter from you at any time you wil write   I am always glad to get letters from friends at home
I remain your affectionate Brother
Wm Coffin to Milton and Deborah

Note: This letter is not dated.
It would appear to be July 24th 1863

I wil send one of Isaacks letters in this   I want them saved til I come home

Wel mother   I wil try to write thee a few lines though I hant any thing of importance to write we are doing tolerable wel here and as wel satisfied as gererally we could be expected for a lot of men to be that are deprived of the comforts of being with their familys and friends   we think we are laboring in a just cause and are willing to take things as they come   I think we wil be likely to be mooved on towards Tuscumbia before long though ant much said about it I have bin thinking of getting some of you to get some honey and butter and send down to me if you can   get honey so it wont cost more than 30 cts a pound against it it gets here   I dont care if you send me a 25 lb can full   the way to send it is to get a tin can made a purpose and put the honey or butter in and have the top soddered on the cans   wil cost $1.00 or 1.50 apiece   if honey is scarce you kneedent to bother about it   if we stay here I would like to have a can of butter and one of honey every two weeks after it gets a little cooler if it dont cost to much to get it here. if it ant to much trouble you may send me a can of each and se what it wil cost   I would like to have some for my own use and the other boys would like to have some and it costs a goodeal more to get it from Dallas   give me the price of butter and honey when you write again   if you send any send it by Adamses express co the express wil

have to be paid before it wil come which wil be 10 or 12 cts a lb   I expect I can pay what butter is worth there and the express and the cost of the can and trouble and sel it to the boys Cheaper than they car buy it here and save myself O C macy has got 3 50 lb cans from Adel   it cost him about 30 cts against he gets it here and he can sell it for 40   I dont know of any thing more to write this time write soon and often and I wil try to answer all letters directed to me
Wm Coffin to Mother

there is a deserter to be shot here tomorrow at 10 oclock   I wil be on picket and wont se it   I dont care about the sight   Luzenah if any of them con-clude to send me some butter and honey you may pay the express and for the cans & C if you have money enough   I guess we wil get pay before long and then I can send you more   the reason I dident write for you to send it was because I know you couldent tend to it wel if aunt hamrer has as much honey as comon tel here I want about 25 lbs a week all fall if we stay here   I want some onions as soon as they get dry enough to box up without spoiling   they are the hardest to get of any thing else down here I wil conclude
I remain as ever yours truly
Wm Coffin to Luzenah

Corinth Miss   July the 25 th 1863

Dear wife   I now take my pen to write you a few lines in answer to your let-ter of 19th and 21st which I have just read and was glad to hear that you war as wel as you was   hope Henry wil be as wel as ever against you get this   I am wel as comon   health in the regiment is about as it has bin for some time we have had very warm weather for a few days   we had a very hard rain this morning it is very warm now and has the appearance of more rain Krysher got a letter from Rachel last evening   they war wel his mother is getting better but not wel yet   we hant had any letters from Anderson since I rote before you neadent to be uneasy about me going out where there is much danger by myself   we always go in squads and take our guns   there is any anount of berrys yet and wil be for some time yet   peaches are getting ripe enough to make good pies   we sold a barrel of pork yesterday and bought a barrel of dried apples so we have fruit of all kinds   you seem to think you wil have to go to fighting pretty soon but I recon you wont   them copperheads are more wxnd than any thing else I think the law if properly executed wil keep them down   their are mean enough to do anything but they are to big cow-ards to carry out their wishes   tel the children I got the flowers they sent me and was glad to get them and to think they thought enough about their pop to think of sending him a present   I would like to send you all a present but I dont know of any thing that I could get to send   tel granny I would like to se

her the best kind   I am sorry to hear of her not being so wel as comon   I
hant had any letter from unkle William lately   there was a man by the name
of A J Johnson in the rebel service   he first was a soldier in the rebel army
was taken prisner at fort Donelson   was kept some time and exchanged and
went back then deserted the rebels and come and joined the 1st Alabama
Cavalry and on the 16th of last June he deserted with a good horse carbine and
saber and good suit of clothes and joined the rebs again   a few days ago he
was caught with some others that had bin trying to burn a railroswd bridge
we was tried and sentenced to be shot which he deserved no doubt   all the
forces at Corinth war marched out to witness the execution   I was on picket
and dident get to se it   I dont suppose it was any pleasant sight   suppose
you wil get an account of the whole affair in the papers more accurate than I
can give so I wil not try to give the details as I wasent an eye witness   I wil
bring my letter to a close by signing, myself
your husband and friend as ever
Wm Coffin To Rachel Luzenah Coffin

Sunday morning   very pleasant dident rain much last night looks as though
it mite rain more yet   I have to go on picket this morning I hant seen Jess
Williams for severel days   guess unkle Jonathan wil be our Regimental
Chaplain our present Chaplain offered his resignation and it is said it has bin
excepted   if so unkle Jonathan wil take the position

tel Benny I would like to have a line from him very wel   tel
all the connection to write when they can and I wil answer
them the best I can   I have quit writing only as I get letters
if any one wants to hear from me all they have to do is to
write no mail
this from your friend Wm Coffin

Corinth   Miss
August the 3rd 1863

Dear wife   I now take my pen to write you a few lines to let you know that I
am wel hopeing those few lines may find you and the children wel I rec your
letter of the 26th last evening and was glad to hear that you was all wel   health
here is about as comon   Krysher ant very wel but stil able to be up   there
is nothing of importance going on here   we have had severel good rains lately
the weather has bin tolerable pleasant for severel days   the weather hant bin
as warm here so far as I expected to se,   wel I would like to have bin there
to have went to Bennys with you   I would like to be with you all the time but
as we cant be together we wil have to do the best we can and wait and trust for

a better time to come   I think the rebs are about plaid out if they dont get for-reign aid soon which I hope they wont   I am glad to hear that the children get along wel with other children for I would hate for them to act like they had to at andersons   I hant had a letter from Dallas for a long time & anderson dont write often to us   the prospect for a crop up there is .gelerelly good from all accounts I guess there wil be rite smart wheat and corn on our place,   I aim to have the wheat ground and hauled to you if there is enough of it to make a load   when you write again tel me how much money you have left I am cooking this week   it ant very hard work but it is tolerable warm work we have fresh pork occasionally   we took in to shoats last week   they come in to our picket post and we take them in out of the wet   we was out guard-ing the mule Carrel one day last week and I killed 3 young squirrels which went off all right   we are not allowed to shoot when we are out that way but I load with little loads that dont make much report   we had a mess of rostenyears yesterday for this first we paid $2.00 for 100 years   every thing of that kind is scarce and very dear onions generally sell for about 5 cts apiece   cucum-bers about 2 cts apiece   young chickens from 30 to 50 cts apiece and other things in proportion I was at negro meeting last knight and heard one old dark-ey preach a very good sermon   they conduct their meetings in a very proper manner Jesse Rosencrats is laying here in the guard house yet he hant had his trial yet   A W Johnson(a brother to A J Johnson that was shot here on the 24th of July) was executed in the same manner and for the same crime on the 21st at memphis that makes 3 of the name since the war begun,   I cant tel any thing about getting a furlow yet   there is 50 or 60 wants furlows and there cant but 3 go at a time so our 3 years wil be out before all wil get so that want to I dont know how I wil come out   I am going to get one if I can   no more this time
I remain your affectionate husband
Wm to Luzenah

Note: There is no date on this letter. It is estimated August 6, 1863

Wel Luzenah   as I have bin writing some to Thol & Abigail I wil write a line to you   we are all doing reasonably wel   got a letter from old Jony Caldwel last evening they war wel Andersons war wel   he said he had cut the grain on our farm said the crop was excelent   the oats was the heaviest he ever raked off of the platform.   he said our sheep was doing wel   he says Wil Frank Davenport is as fat as a cub   O C Macy got a letter from Levi Davis stating that at a meeting in Adel when the preacher was praying he prayed for the suc-cess of ar army   old john davenport was down on his old bones but when it come to praying for success to our army he jumped up so mad he could bite

himself.   I wish some boddy had have shot him to prevent him from haveing
any more such sins to answer for   the old boy wil get all such christians
unless they change their ways   Dave Clark has got home   he cut my rye on
the shares   I expect he ant much better off than we was before he went to the
peak   after dinner and the dishes washed and I wil finish my letter   Krysher
is pretty sick today but I guess it wont last long   I rote to mother for some of
them to send me some butter and honey if they could bother about it   I dont
care much about butter this time of the year if honey is plenty   I would like
to have a can when you write tel whether honey is plenty and what it is worth
& C   I dont know of any thing more to write this time so I wil conclude this
from your affectionate husband
Wm Coffin To R L Coffin

I got a letter from Nathan last evening   tell him I wil write to him soon   tel
henry and Sis I want to hear from them how much they have learnt what they
have done with their pet squirrels & C   tel them I want them to get their mother to write me a good letter for them & they could compose a pretty good letter   no more to Luzenah

Sunday evening   August the 9th 1863

Dear wife   I now take my pen to write you a few lines   received your letter of the 2nd & 3rd last evening   I was glad to.hear that you and the children was wel but sorrow to hear of the rest being so afflicted   I hope they
wil all be better before this reaches you   I am wel as comonWeir & Krysher
are stil grunting but both able to be up and about   health about as comon
generally   there is nothing of any importance being done here lately   we
had a prize drill yesterday   the two best companys out of each regiment in
our Brigade drilled   our co was choosed one of the two best in our Regt but
we dident drill on account of our officers all being sick   the other company
had one days notice and their officers to drill them   Colonel Redfield acted the
dog with us we dident want to go but he wouldent excuse us and never got us
an officer to command us til we war formed in line to start giveing us no time
to train any   under the Lieutenant that went out with us we went through
inspection but dident drill   Col Redfield the old dog instead of telling the
truth told the inspectors and judges that it was our own fault that we dident
come out in better style that we had due notice & C   he was a mity good man
til he got to commanding the Regt   since then he has bin getting meaner every
day   you needent to send any butter down here if you dont have it bought
before you get this   I would like wel enough to have the honey if you can get
it handy   I dont want you to put your self to any extra trouble about it   dont
know when we wil get paid again   I guess that it was the paymasters that was

to pay this division that was on the boat that was destroyed some time ago with fire   I wil get the wheat ground and hauled to you but you buy flour to do til you get it   I dont want you to feed the children on cornbread when they cant hardly eat it at all   I want you and them to to have plenty to eat and wear as long as you have money to by with   I have just finished my weeks cooking today   we take it week about all round   I always get ready to qvit against the week is out   it is to confineing for me   we have had a nice shower this evening   the negroes are carrying on a protracted meeting in about 300 yards of here   I was over night before last and am going again to night   they have some very good preachers   we dont have meeting in the regiment very often on account of haveing no suitable place   I wil close for this time   write when convenient   take as good care of your self as you can for I would hate to hear of you getting sick
I remain your affectionate husband and friend
Wm Coffin to R. L Coffin

friday evening   August 14th 1863

Dear wife   I take my pen to write you a few lines though I dont know that I have any thing of much importance to write   I am wel as comon and hope when this reaches you it wil find you wel   I received your letter of the 5th last evening and was glad to hear that the rest war getting better but sorry to hear that you had a sore foot so you couldent walk but I hope it wil be better before you get this   write and tel what is the matter with it   I was out in the coun-try 11 miles yesterday   there was 25 of us went out with two teams to get apples   we dident find them very plenty but got enough to do the Regiment 2 or 3 days   we got what peaches we could eat but none worth any thing to bring in   I have bin washing and patching some today   I can wash very wel but patching is rather out of my line of business   I like the way the home guard served the copperhead   that wil make them think what war is like and maybe they wont be so keen to do all they can to extend this war   I would be glad to hear of some more of them taking the oath in the same way   tel granny I got the candy she sent me   I was glad to get a present from her   tel her I would like to send her a present if I had any thing that I could send but I hant and dont know as I can get any thing   I am glad to hear that she is able to go to meeting and to Briton & C   tel her I hant seen Jess lately   he was over to se me a day or to ago but I was out on picket   Weir and Krysher are both complaining yet but stil able to be up and about   Mack Coons hant bin able for duty but a few days in the last 4 months   the mail has come and I got a letter from father   tel him I wil answer it soon I dont want any of you to go to any trouble about sending me any butter   if you can send me a can of honey I would be glad   we can get butter here now for 35cts and it wil cost nearly that to get it from Iowa   I wil quit for this time write when convenient

I remain your affectionate husband
W Coffin To R L Coffin

Note: There is no date on this letter. It was probably written about August 19, 1863.

Dear wife   I thought I would write you a few lines though I hardly know what to write   I got a letter from Anderson yesterday   they war all wel Anderson writes that they had a good rain the night of the 26th   he sais corn wont be very good the wheat and oats was good on our farm and he says the corn is better than it is on his   our bees swarmed when they war away from home and the children let them go off   diner has a colt anderson writes that it is a very good colt about the color of george except it has a blaze face   he said it was doing wel tel Sis it wil be her little horse as long as her george horse died   Krysher is up and about but not very stout   their is complaining but nothing serious the matter I guess.   I wit conclude for want of something to write about
I remain your affectionate husband
Wm Coffin To Luzenah

you rote about a revolver   I couldent send you one if I had it nothing of that kind is allowed to be shiped   dont hardly think you wil nead one   I think there is certainly patriotism and spunk enough in the north yet to not allow women imposed upon to to great an extent

Sunday August the 23 1863

Dear wife   I once more take my pen to drop you a few lines   I am wel as comon and hope this wil find you wel   I received your letter of the 13th last evening   I was glad to hear that you and the children stil keep wel   we hant bin paid off yet but it is generally believed that we wil be in a week or so   I guess we wil get 52 dollars   there wil be $78 comeing to us the 1st of September but I dont expect we wil get but 4 months pay this time   wel I wil tel you something about the furlow business   we have drawed for the next three lots and I dident happen to be any one of the lucky men the first 3 are looking for their furlows to come on this evening Weir gets to go in the 2nd lot it wil take about 4 months for the 3 lots to go and get back then we wil draw again   I wil stand an equal chance with 40 others which is rather a slim chance but somebody wil be lucky and I have as good a chance as any   the captain did talk of letting all the married men go first but the young men raised

56

such a fuss and contended that they had as good a rite to a furlow as married men so he let all draw out of the 9 that get to go next   5 of them are single men   I stil feel in hopes we wil all get to go home in 12 months   I dont want you to put yourselves to to much bother about sending me that honey   as to the butter I dont care any thing about it   I can buy plenty here about as cheap as I can get it from there   if you have got the cans and hant got the butter and can get honey I would rather you would send all honey but if you have got the butter send it I can make use of it   I dont know of any thing more to write this time so I wil close for the present and write a few lines to mother write as often as convenient

your husband affectionately

Wm Coffin to Wife and children

the 7th Iowa with the rest of the 1st Brigade went to Lagrange this week

Dear mother   I wit try to write thee a few lines though I dont know of any thing to write that would be likely to interest thee   I was glad to hear that thee was getting up and about again I got a letter from unkle Wm Mills last evening they war all wel when he rote   unkle Jonathan Rolls and very Stout   he has offered his resignation   I dont know whether it wil be excepted or not. I dont want you to furnish honey or butter to send down here to me   I am able to buy such things all I wanted was for some of you to help Luzenah about fixing it up and starting it   we have never heard from the prisners that was taken from the corell since they left Tuscumbia   I wil quit for this time write often

I remain thy son as ever

Wm Coffin

Friday evening
August the 28th 1863

Dear wife   I now take my pen to write you a few lines in answer to your letter of the 20th which I received last evening   I was glad to hear that you and the children stil keep wel for health is one of the greatest blessings this world can afford   I am wel as comon at present the health of our Company is as good as it has bin at any time since we left Iowa   we are on picket about 3 times a week since the first brigade left but that is all the duty we have to do we dont drill any   we have had very cool weather for 3 or 4 days I think it has bin as cool as I ever saw in Iowa at this season of the year   when you start the butter and honey to me write me a letter so I wil know when to look for it   there is nothing much going on about here   the guerrillas stil keep doing some mischief around here but it dont amount to much   they get took in every once in awhile   there is stil deserters Combing in here every few

days and from all accounts there is lots deserting and going in at other places the rebel army must be in an awful condition   I think they are about once through though it may be some time yet before they give it up   I understand that they wont trust Tennesse soldiers on picket any more   if that be the case they certainly cant depend on them much to fight   Tennessee is sending lots of men in to our army   there was a portion of the 1st west Tenn cavalry went up through tennessee a few days ago to recruit they war gone 10 days and got 70 white recruits and 50 negroes that is as good as could be done in any northern state   I guess the copperheads had as wel begin to draw in their horns for their cause like that of rebels in the South is hopeless   it is reported that the paymaster come on the train this evening and I guess it is so if he did we wil get paid in 2 or 3 days   I shal send what I send to you by express to Fairfield I shant send but 30 or 35 dollars we wil get 52   I want to keep some for expence money and enough to pay my way if I get a chance to go home on a furlow   if I get a furlow it wil cost me $30 or 35 to make the trip   the boys thats to go next have bin waiting some time to get their money   they hadent money enough to bare their expenses til they get paid off Hi Moffett our chief musician is discharged on account of his health   he wil start home Monday there has bin 11 men discharged and 11 died from our co since it was first organized and 8 taken prisner,   tel granny I am glad to hear that she is stil able to go to meeting   I would like to send her a nice peach if there was any chance tel henry and sis that I would like to be there to help them gather plumbs   tel them I want them to be good children and help their mother all they can   I wil quit for this time write when convenient
I remain your affectionate husband and friend
Wm Coffin To Rachel L Coffin

Corinth Miss Sept the 1st 1863

Dear wife   I now take my pen to write you a few lines in answer to your letter of the 25 of August which I red a day or to ago   I was glad to hear that you and the children stil kept wel   I am wel as comon we have had very cool weather for severel days but it is warmer today   you wanted to know how I was going to get the flour hauled to you   I am going to let Anderson hire somebody to haul it to you   I dont expect to haul it myself   if I get a furlow anytime this winter I dont expect to go to Dallas atall   old Peter R Russel landed here last Sunday evening   he wil preach in one of our shantys tonite for the first time since he come down   our three boys that got furlows and Hi Moffet started home last Sunday morning   I am cooking this week   I get things up in flamin stile as A Mard would say   we bought 10 bushels of green beens last saturday   we got the whole pile for $2.00   the cheapest of anything ever sold in dixey   I guess I baked a big corn pone last nite   it was the best corn bread I have tasted since I left Iowa.   we dont often get any meal here we hant had a better from Dallas lately   we got our pay today we got $52   I have paid Krysher and O C Macy paid me   I want you to send me his note in the next letter you send   be careful and have the letter backed plain I am going to send you thirty dollars by express   I wil start it in a day or to I wil direct it to you   tel Phebe I wil get her boy a new dress when I se it if I think it is good enough looking to deserve it   tel granny I would like to be there to go plumbing with her and the children   I would like to se their little toe heads jumping around after plumbs I wil quit for this time   I dont expect you can read what I have rote   write often   Wm Coffin To R L Coffin

wel Mother   I wil try to write thee a few lines   we are all getting along as wel as ever soldiers did   unkle Jonathan ant very stout yet   there was 6 or 8 rebels or guerrillas made a dash on our negro pickets nite before last   the negroes killed one of the villains so they say   I heard the fireing it sounded like they war fighting a battle   am going to send the 2 or 3 grapes so the can get the seed   they ant ripe yet but the seed wil grow   I believe they call them fox grapes   they grow in the woods   I dont want the to fret about the butter and honey   I am doing fine   I dident expect you to furnish it in the first place I wil quit for this time   write often   tel the rest if they want to hear from me they can do so by writing to me   I have quit writing unless I get letters I remain as ever Wm Coffin To Mother

Corinth Miss
Sunday Evening   Sept the 6th 1863

Dear Wife   I this evening take any pen to write you a few lines   I am wel as comon and hope when this reaches you it wil find you and the children wel the health of the boys is about as comon   Weir is stout   Krysher is up and about but not stout   he hant bin able for duty but very little of the time since we come here   Mack Coons about the same way   there is talk now of both of them and little Jeff Wright getting discharged   I hope they wil for I hate to se a man kept here that ant able for the service and no prospect of them getting able   old Peter Y Russell preached at 11 today and at 3 he preach the funerel of a man in Co D that died last night   we hant had any letters from Dallas since I rote   I started $35 to you on the 2nd by express   I am going to send henry a gun so he can fight copperheads   tel sis I wil send her a present as soon as I can get one suitable for her   there is stil some guerrillas taken in every few days and occasionally some of our men get taken in by them there is no prospect of us leaving here that I know of   we have had very pleas-

ant weather for some time   I dont know yet when Macy wil get the wheat thrashed so I can send you the flour   I want you to by what you kneed til you get it   let it be long or short I have it hauled to you as soon as I can get it done   I cant think of any thing more to write this time so I wil conclude by asking you to write often
this from your affectionate husband
William Coffin To Rachel Coffin

I wil send Sis a spade

Note: There is no date on this letter. It was probably written September 13, 1863

I am going over to negro meeting today   we dont have meetings very regular here lately   there is no very suitable place to accomodate many   I expect the folks up there call me an abolitionist   if they do all right   it is an honor to be called an Abolitionist to what it is to be a copperhead.   I clam to be a full blooded Abolitionist now   I fully endorse the Presidents emancipation proclamation under the present circumstances and think all loyal people wil do the same against they se what I have already seen   I want to se the negroes free and fighting their masters til they come to honorable terms of peace   you write that you have to take a goodeal on my account   I hope there ant many such lowlifed villans that have no more principal than to insult a woman   I want you to mark them all down   I hope you wil be able to bear up under your trials and never once wish me a copperhead so I could be with you   I would rather die here and leave an honorable name for you and the children the to live a thousand years a copperhead to disgrace the comeing geneations no more
yours with love and repect I sign my name as ever
W C

be of good cheer under all circumstances if posible

Corinth Miss   Sept the 15th 1863

Dear wife   I once more take my pen to write you a few lines to let you know that I am wel and doing wel   I rec your letter of the 8th a evening before last and was glad to hear that you and the children stil kept wel   I got the can of honey to day   it came through all right   I sold the most of it to the boys I sold at 40 cts a pound   I thought that would about pay expenses I could

sold just as easy at 50 but I dident want to speculate off of the boys   I kept about 4 lbs for my own use   I want you to write what the honey cost a lbs and what the cans cost apiece and what the express is & C so I can tel what I can afford to sel at if thou send any more   I sold $6.50 worth out of this can, you may send the other can when ever you can convenient   ant in any hurry, tel Nathan or Jim or any of them that if they wil fix up a can every 2 weeks and send I wil pay them wel for their trouble   I would rather have strained honey the come all mashes up by the time it gets here   write in your next letter and tel me whether honey is plenty   what it is worth & C   I dont want you to bother about sending any more   it is to much work for you   if they send any tel them to get 50 lb cans if they can   tel henry he is biger than his pop if he has got new boots for I hant had a pair since I left home   tel him he must not dirty the heels of them we got a letter from Anderson a few days ago they war tolerable wel   the mail has just come   I got a letter from ander-son   they war all wel   they have got the wheat and oats thrashed   there was 52 bus of wheat and 80 of oats to my share   he thinks they wil be to busy to haul that flour   if there is any of the boys in jefferson that want to haul it I wil give them $1.00 per hundred   there wil be 17 or 18 hundred of what my wheat wil make   I wil get enough to make 20 or 25 hundred if they should want to haul that much   if they dont any of them want the job write to me and I wil have Anderson to hire somebody else   I wil have the wool hauled to you when the flour is hauled   I wrote to anderson that he could have the place next year   I thought I had better rent while I had a chance Caldwells wants the wool and let us have as much next year   I dont know but it would be a good idea as it is getting late and likely would be some trouble to get it carded   write and let me know whether you want it or whether I had bet-ter let them have it and get it all together next year   I wil have it arranged to suit you if I can   be sure and write next time about it   we have settled for our first years clothing my bill was $45.00 all over $42 wil come out of our next pay   it wont take near that much to keep us the next year   I have enough clothes to do me 6 months   I wil quit for this time   write often
I remain your affectionate husband as ever
William Coffin

Saturday Sept the 26th

Dear wife   I now take my pen to write you a few lines in answer to yours of the 13th which I received last evening and was glad to hear that you and the children was wel   I am wel as comon the boys are generally wel   we have many men in the hospital from our Co   it is the first time we could say so since we got here   the weather is stil cool   it frosted last nite again   the cotton is injured til there wont be over a half crop   we can get all the sweet potatoes we want by paying $2.00 per bushel for them there ant any more

prospect of us leaveing here than there was when I rote before   we hant had a letter from Andersons lately   I wil write to them today about the wool   I want you to write whether any of the boys want to haul that flour or not. there was a negro come in yesterday that has bin a prisner with Cap Loomis at Tuscumbia   Cap is sent to Richmond to be exchanged   you needent to send that honey til I write again   if you hant started it yet   if you have the honey keep it   I dont know of any thing more to write this time.   write often tel granny I would like to have the chance to lay with her little bedfellow   tel Sis she musent hug her dol to much   tel henry he must be a good boy and learn to spel as fast as he can   I wil close
I am your friend and husband as ever
Wm Coffin

Note: This letter has been partially destroyed. Word or letters within (parenthesis) are an attempt to reconstruct the missing words.

Lagrange   Tennesse Oct the 15th 1863

Dear wife   I now take my pen to write you a few lines in ans (wer) to your letter of the 6th which (I rec) today and was glad to(hear)that you was wel   (I am as)wel as common   the (boys are) generally wel (We left) Corinth last Sunday (morning at) about 8 oclock and got(here) about two that knight (wel we we) have bin here since(we) come here to hold the (p)lace wile the troops that was here went out after some rebs that undertook to do some mischief down at Coliersville   our forces are reported to be close after them   we are in the quarters(of) the 2nd Iowa they are out (with) the 7th   I think we wil (be back to Corinth as soon (as our) troops come back that belongs here   I got a letter from Anderson yesterday   they war all wel   he has sold my part of the corn for 15 cts a bus   I wrote to him to get the fl(our) hauled if he could if no(t) sel the wheat and send (you) the money so you could (   )   there is stil troops passi(ng by) east every day this is(a very) nice place and has an   ( ) a rich place   tel Hen(ry I was) glad to hear that he (is a big) boy to work tel him I (would be) glad to se (if hes as) big as pop yet   tel sis I (was glad) to hear that she is a(good) girl   I hope she wil al(ways) be a good girl I would(be) glad to se them and you to   Walt Garoutte brings the word that unkle henrys got their old house burnt while he was at home and all their wheat

62

and a goodeal of other property   I wil quit for I have a poor chance write
often   I wil write if we are order(ed) any where else
I remain y(our) affectionate wife as ever
Wm Coffin

Corinth Miss
Oct the 19th 1863

Dear wife   I this evening take my pen to write you a few lines in answer to
your letter of the 12th which I just rec   I am wel as comon   we just got
back this evening   we marched back from Lagrange   it was 2 1/2 days hard
marching   stood the trip very wel   it rained nearly all night the first night we
was out   the most of the boys got wet soaked flat   Mount and I made a tent
out of our gum blankets that kept us dry   it is 45 miles from here to Lagrange
by railroad and about 60 the way we come   it was the crookedest road I ever
saw   we found things all right here there was another regt in our quarters
while we was gone but they took good care of our things, and left all in good
order   the troops are stil going east as fast as the cars can take them   I think
we wil be likely to stay here a while   I wish you would knit me a couple of
pair of socks and send to me when you send the honey   if you can get the
yarn to knit them out of I can get plenty of socks here but they ant much
account you neadent to send them til I write to you to   if you send the honey
you can put the socks in the box around the can   was going to send you a box
of percimons and chesnuts while we was at Lagrange but I dident have time
I got some percimons but dident have time to box them up   wil send you a few
beech nuts in this letter for I expect you never saw any   the train that Krysher
is in is gone   they left while we was gone   Jesse Rosencrants our deserter has
had his trial and was sentanced to imprisonment in the military prison at Alton
Ills for his time of enlistment   it is rather hard but nothing more than he
deserved   if a man goes to serve his country I like to se him do it like a man
I cant think of any thing to write to interest you and it is about bed time and I
haunt slept very wel for a week so I wil quit and go to bed this is the 20 and I
wil finish my letter   I have bin washing this fore noon   I done 50 cts worth
of washing besides my own, I guess I wont send any more money by mail   I
wil keep it til we are paid again and send it all together unless you kneed some
if you kneed any or are likely to kneed any write and I wil send you some at
any time   no more
yours as ever
Wm Coffin

Corinth Oct the 27th

Dear Wife   I this evening take my pen to write you a few lines   I am wel as comon and hope this wil find you and the children wel   the boys are generally wel   O C Macy is sick with the jaunders and eresipelas   he ant very sick   Krysher got back to the company a day or to ago   he is tolerable stout again   we drawed 2 months pay yesterday got I got $22.85 cts   I had taken up $3.15 cts for clothes more than is allowed a year   it wont take near that much to do me tho next year   I wil start some money to you in a few days by express   I wit write to you when I start its   the talk now is that we wil leave here friday or Saturday   I dont know where we are to go to   we have no marching orders yet and maybe we wont get at all   there is always so many rumors that we never now what to believe   I wil write to you as soon as we find out whether we wil leave or not   I cant think of any thing more to write at present so I wil close by asking you to write often

I remain your affectionate husband

Wm Coffin To R L Coffin

Sunday evening
Nov the 1st

I dident get this done in time to send it last nite and I thought I would write a little more   we have had a very nice day but I believe it has bin the lonesomest day to me that I have had since I have bin in the service   there is no more orders yet about leaveing we are looking for orders all the time to leave Capt. Rippey of co E died evening before last   his remains war started home this morning   I wil quit for this time   I wil write again before we leave here

I remain your loveing husband as ever

4 oclock Monday morning
November the 2nd 1863

Dear wife   I take my pen to write you a few lines though I just started a letter to you yesterday we are ordered to be ready to leave at 8 oclock this morning   we wil go on the cars to Iuka   if we go further than there we wil have to foot it   I wil write again as soon as find where we are likely to go to   I want you to write often and I wil write to you unless we get out to where we have no mail   letters wil come to us if there is any chance at all   breakfast is about ready and I wit have to quit for this time

I remain your affectionate husband

Wm Coffin

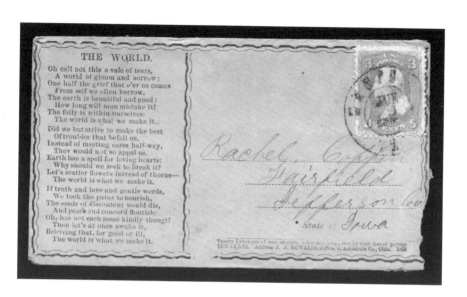

THE WORLD.

Oh call not this a vale of tears,
    A world of gloom and sorrow;
One half the grief that o'er us comes
    From self we often borrow.
The earth is beautiful and good:
    How long will man mistake it?
The folly is within ourselves:
    The world is what we make it.

Did we but strive to make the best
    Of troubles that befall us,
Instead of meeting cares half-way,
    They would not so appal us.
Earth has a spell for loving hearts:
    Why should we seek to break it?
Let's scatter flowers instead of thorns—
    The world is what we make it.

If truth and love and gentle words,
    We took the pains to nourish,
The seeds of discontent would die,
    And peace and concord flourish:
Oh, has not each some kindly thought?
    Then let's at once awake it,
Believing that, for good or ill,
    The world is what we make it.

Twenty Envelopes of various sizes, colors and prices, sent by mail free of postage
TEN CENTS. Address J. A. BOWELLS, Jefferson, Ashtabula Co., Ohio. 1862

Rachel Coffin
Fairfield
Jefferson Co
• *State of Iowa*

Mrs Rachel Coffin
Pleasant Plain
Jefferson Co
Iowa

Family Photo circa 1880
Back row: Cora Coffin, Henry Coffin, and Malinda Coffin
Front row: Rachel Coffin, William Coffin, and Jennie Coffin

Family Portrait:
Back row: Jennie Coffin Cornelison, Henry Coffin
Front row: Rachel Coffin, Malinda Coffin McNichols, and Wm Coffin

Grandmother and Granddaughter:
Cora Lavona Cornelison Chapman with grandmother Rachel Coffin
Approximately 1917

"Grandchildren"
68th Wedding Anniversary, Sept. 3, 1925

68th Anniversary of Coffin parents and children, September 3, 1925
Rachel Coffin, Malinda McNichols, Henry Coffin, Jennie Cornelison, and Wm Coffin

Rachel & William Coffin

Old soldiers in Soldiers Home at Tacoma, Washington. Sent to Wm Coffin from his nephew Wm Coffin of Tacoma

Coffin Sisters Millenary — Circa 1900 —Adel, Iowa
From left: unknown woman, Cora Coffin, and Jennie Coffin

in the woods on richland creek Jarrals Co Tenn Nov the 14th 1863

Dear wife   I this morning take my pen to write you a few lines I am wel at present and hope this wil find you wel   we left Iuka on the morning of the 6th we marched 9 miles to east port on the Tenn. river   by noon crossed and marched all that after noon and half the night unloading boats   the 7 we started on   we stoped here the evening of the   we saw nothing on the road worth mentioning   no towns worth any thing til we got to Pulaski 9 miles south of here   it is the county seat of garrels Co   it is a very nice place   we are stationed on the nashville and Decator Railroad   our regt is scattered along for some distance   there is only 4 Co here   I guess it is the calculation to open the railroad   our brigade is ordered to forage enough horses and mules to mount one Co in each regiment   we war out yesterday and got 20 or 30 head   we went to get a lot the rebs had hid in a hollow but they smelt a mice and mooved them   we took one prisner   we had hid oat in the woods and tied up his horse and laid down and went to sleep   we got rite up to him before he waked we found 5 horses tied in the woods   I dont know how long we wil stay here   probably severel days   we hant had any mail yet since we left Iuka   we are fixed here so we can live tolerable comfortable   we have to depend mostly on foraging for our liveing   the is a rich country   the people have plenty of amost every thing   I have a very poor chance to write so I wil close for the present   I guess we wil get mail regular in a few days write often I wil write as often as once a week if we stay where we have a chance to send letters out
I remain your affectionate husband as ever
Wm Coffin To R L Coffin

Jarrels   Co   Tenn Nov the 16th 1863

Dear wife   I this evening take my pen to try to write you a few lines in answer to your letter of the 1st which I rec last evening   I was glad to hear that you and the children was wel   I am wel as comon   we are stil where we first stoped and likely we wont go far   from here soon   they are repairing this railroad and it wil have to be guarded and we are as likely to stay here as any body our Co is to be mounted on mules and horses   we have about half enough mules and horses now and we aim to go out tomorrow to try and get the rest   we took a little scout this evening and got 3 good horses and 2 mules the most of the boys are very wel pleased with the idea of being mounted   for my part I dont care much about it any way you wanted to know what Anderson had done with the money the corn come to   he hadent got the money when he wrote to me he wil send it to you when he gets it   I sent you $40.00 before I left Corinth which I suppose you have got before this time I rote to anderson to sel the wheat and send you the money if he couldent get the flour hauled to you   I dont want you to think I dont intend to keep you in money plenty for as long as I live and it is in my power I expect for you to have plen-ty   I want you to spend all the money that is necessary to make you and the children comfortable I dident keep but little money myself

but if I get out I can borrow til pay day   I hant seenKrysher since we left Corinth   he come along as we did but the train was so long the we never seen lots of regiments at all when we war on the road marching   our train was 25 or 30 miles long Krysher is at Columbia about 32 miles north of here   we hant heard from the boys we left at Corinth since we left   we hant had but one mail since we come here   our mail wil be unregular for awhile   the mail only comes and goes as troops pass backward and forward   we are live-ing fat we have all the beef mutton and fresh pork chicken turkey sweet pota-toes & C that we can use   our quarters ant quite as good as mite be   we have no tents   only what we make out of our gum blankets   they keep us dry but we have to get down and crawl in them   this the 17th very warm and pleas-ant   we aim to start by sun up this morning to try and get some more horses and mules we had a turkey for breakfast this morning and mush fried in the gravy   our worst trouble is to get vesels to cook in   we dident fetch many with us   I must quit and get ready to straddle my mule good by for this time
Wm Coffin

this is a very hilly country but it is very rich   the people here have plenty of everything   when people talk of starving the rebel out they talk about some-thing that cant hardly be done the woods is full of the nicest kind of hogs they are fat on the most   there is the most beech most here I ever saw any where the ground is covered   our regiment is scattered all over the country they are running two mils   we just take possesion of every thing we kneed and use it to suit our selves   we give receipts for all property to be settled at the close of the war   if we get this road in runing order to decator that wil nearly split the confederacy in to again   I think if we have good luck for the next 6 mo the confederacy wil be about gave up   I expect I have scratched more than you can read   have a very poor chance to virite if you cant read it write and let me know and I wil try and take a little more pains next time   no more this time I remain your affectionate husband
Wm Coffin

Tenn Nov the 24th 1863

Dear wife   I this morning take my pen to write you a few lines I am wel as
comon and hope this wil find you wel   hant had but one letter from you since
we got here   I dont think our mail comes as it ought to   we get a little mail
nearly every day but we dont get near as much as we ought to   it is raining
this morning and looks as though it mite rain some time   our Co was all
ordered out yesterday that had saddles   I was on picket and dident get to go
there was 20 men and the Cap went out   they war ordered to take 3 days
rations in their haversacks   there is no telling where they wil go or when they
wil be back   we have horses and mules enough to mount the Co but we lack
a good many saddles and bridles yet we hant heard from the boys we left at
Corinth yet Weir Couch is in the hospital   he has a very bad cough a goodeal like he had last winter   he is so as to be up and about the most of the time
Krysher passed here the other day with his team   he was wel   the citizens
around here are getting very loyal for the sake of saving their property   we
hant had any news since we left Corinth   we dont get any papers   if peace
was declared I dont expect we would find it out soon   there was a negro stole
a guerrillers horse last night and fetched him in this morning just at daylight
the negroes are the only people in this country that we can depend on there is
some good white men but we cant tel who they are all the time   there was a
negro shot his overseer night before last in the guts   they sent for our doctor
he says he thinks he can cut him off above and below the wound and put him
together so he wit be all right   tel the children I would like to send them
something but there is nothing here that I can get to send them   I would like
to se them and you to the best kind   I do hope the time wil soon come when
we can all return to our familys and friends and live in peace and harmony as
we did before this wicked and causeless rebelion   I dont know of any thing
more to write this time so I wil close by requesting you to write often
I remain your affectionate husband
Wm Coffin To R L Coffin

this is the 25th   the boys got back yesterday at noon   they only went to
Columbia to guard the mail there and back we had then to go down to Pulaski
with it in the afternoon   today was was out 5 miles to where Co A is   they
keep us scouting around nearly all the time   I got your letter of the 9th yesterday it had bin 16 days on the road   our mail dont seem to come strait from
some cause you seem to complain that you dont get letters regular   I rote 2
just before we left Corinth and two at Iuka and this makes 3 since we got here
I dident write any on the road for I dident have time nor we dident have any
chance to send letters   we are signing the pay rolls this evening   we wil get
2 mo pay in a few days I   dont expect to send you any at the present as there
is no express line here and the mail seems to be pretty uncertain   I think

Anderson wil send you some money before long   I want you to write and let me know whether you got the $40 I sent you from Corinth or not if you are likely to get out of money at any time write and I wil send you some by mail we hant heard from the sick boys at Corinth yet   I hant heard from Weir today tel Henry and sis I would like to be there to eat parched corn with them   I cant think of any thing more to write this time so I wil quit and write some to Cas
I remain your affectionate husband as ever
Wm Coffin To R L Coffin

tel Dick I am glad he is able to keep his forked end down   I think he is doing wel not to get married or go to war either   tel him to write me a letter

Dec the 6th 1863

Dear Wife   I this evening take my pen to write you a few lines in answer to your letters of the 15th & 20th of last month   I was glad to hear that you stil kept wel   I am wel as comon we have just got in off of a 7 days scout   we started last monday morning   we went back towards Corinth about 65 miles and then took out through the country I would have rote to you before we started but I dident have time after we got orders   I rec you letter of the 15th at Linville after we started   we war out with 6 companys of the 50th Ills one of the 7th and 4 of the 18th Missouri   we dident have any fight   we got 25 or 30 prisners   we only had one shot fired at us while we was out and that dident hurt anybody   we wounded one reb   dident kill any one   we got severel good horses mules negroes & C   we had a very nice trip except 2 or 3 of the first days it was rather cool   I like riding better than lugging a knapsack   we got to see rite smart of the country   I seen some of the rock that we read off I saw rock 100 feet rite strait up   we war in a rich country   we allways camped with secesh   I expect we made severel of them think darn it when we war pitching in to their corn cribs oats hay foder hog hens chicken roosts bee hives & C   we lived like kings   wel I have just bin to hear old peter preach   it is the first chance I have had to hear preaching since I left Corinth   he has preached 2 or 3 times but I was always on duty   there was 4 women at meeting the first I have saw at meeting since I left Corinth home   they war citizens that live close here we are building quarters here I think we will stay here some time Mat Noel and O D Russell have just got here they left O C Macy at Mound City Ills   he wasent very sick but not able to come to the Regt   O D has got stout again   I hant bin to se Weir yet   the boys say he is getting along very   wel the rest of the boys are wel except cold   I got a letter from Andersons they war wel   oel is married to Rachel Sheriden   they write as though unkle henry mills was stil aiming to haul you some flour   I am going to write to Anderson to give Joel $20 in something he has done a goodeal of work for me and I always aimed to give him and Weir something and I expect he kneeds it as bad now as he ever wil   I got a letter from unkle Wm Mills today   they war wel   he says crops was poor except wheat and grain was very high Anderson writes that they are about ready to moove in their new house Joel is going to live in the old one   you may use that honey if you want to   it ant likely there wil be any chance to get it here soon   you may keep the sock til I write for you to send them   I bought 2 pair since I came here they cost 75 cts a pair   I have signed for about $25 on this years account Krysher is back to his Co   he is as fat as a bear   I have wrote about all I can think of at present and I guess you wont complain of it not being long enough   tel Henry and sis I want them to learn their books and be good children   tel them that pop has got a big black horse that can run over comon horses and never brake his gait   I wil quit for this time   write often if I dont write you may know it is because I hant the chance

yours as ever

Wm Coffin to R L Coffin

This is the 7th

and it is a very nice day   I have bin up to the hospital to se Weir he is getting along very wel   unkle Jonathan got here last knight   he ant stout but better than when we leftt Corinth   we hant bin paid off yet but I guess we wil soon I wil quit for this time

I remain your affectionat husband as ever

Wm Coffin To R L Coffin

Dec the 12th 1863

Dear Wife

I this morning take my pen to write you a few lines   I arn tolerable wel at present   I received your letter of the 29th of nov a day or to ago and hant had a chance to answer it til now   Weir is getting along very wel   he wil soon be able for duty if he keeps mending   Mat Mount went to the hospital yesterday he hant bin rite wel since we left Corinth   there is severel of the boys complaining more or les   Krysher has got back to the Co   he is as fat as a bear   we have turned our mules over to the 50th Ills so when wil go now we wil go a foot and I am glad of it   I liked scouting very wel but they kep us going so study that it was very hard on us   we hardly got a good knights sleep while we was mounted   we got paid off a few days ago   we got $26 I dont aim to send any home this time unless you get to kneeding some   I bought me an overcoat that cost $7.00 and I had borrowed some so I couldent send much ifI was to send all I could spare   I want you to stil writehow much you have

on hand and if you are likely to get out at any time I wil send you some   I
dont get any word from Anderson about what is due me up there   I wrote to
himto let Joel have $20 worth of something if there was any thing in the place
that he neaded   if not to let him have $10 in money he has done a goodeal
of work for me and never got much for it and I thought likely he neaded a little help now as bad as he ever would we are building quarters here the most of
the Companys have got their houses up we war kep so busy while we war
mounted that we hadent time to build there is some talk of us leaveing here in
2 or 3 weeks though there is nothing certain about it   we never know when
we are going to moove til we start   we have had a goodeal of rainy weather
lately and it is raining now   there is a heap of cotton in this country   they
are hauling it to market by the wholesale   there is a goodeal of the present
crop not picked yet the darkys have all went and rund away and there ant any
body to pick it   you kneedent to send them socks yet   the mail is so uncertain I have bought two new pair of homemade socks   I had to pay 75cts a
pair   you may use the honey if you can if not keep it til vou can   I am going
to send you a half dollar and the children a quarter apiece for a Christmas gift
if you get it in time you can buy what ever you.plese with it I cant think of any
thing more at present so I wil close by requesting you to write often
I stil remain your affectionate husband as ever
W Coffin To R L Coffin & the children

I wish you would send me a dollars worth of postage stamps   we cant get
any here

Camp Redfield   Giles Co Tenn
Dec 21st 1863

Dear Wife I this evening take my pen to write you a few lines to let you know
how I am getting along I am wel as comon I received your letter of the 12th
this evening I was glad to hear that you was getting better I was very uneasy
til I got your letter this evening   I hope by the time you get this you wil be
wel we have got our houses up and in them   we are fixed to live tolerable
comfortable if we get to stay here   Weir has left the hospital but he ant able
for duty yet Mat Mount is stil in the hospital   he dont mend very fast   I got
a letter from O C Macy today he is in the general hospital at Mound City Ills
he is mending slowly there   unkle Jonathan Rolls is stil in the hospital   he
dont mend very much   it ant likely he wil ever be stout again   the cars hant
got to runing here yet   the talk is that it wil be 6 weeks before they run here
tedl sis I am glad that she slil keeps able to sing tel her I want her to learn so
she can sing to pop when he comes home   tel henry I would like to se his toe
head and wool him around awile   one of our men whiped an old secesh the

other day   a fair fist fight   he had beat one of his negroes unmercifully and the soldier asked him if he wasent ashamed and he got very saucy and told him he would beat his negroes when he pleased   the soldier pounded him til he blated like a calf he let his darkys do as they please since that   I have nothing of importance to write so I wil close
I stil remain your ever wel wishing husband
Wm Coffin To R L Coffin

Christmas after dinner   1863

Dear Wife
I embrace the present as as suitable apportunity to write you a few lines to let you know how I am getting along   I am wel at present and and hope this wil find you and the children wel   the boys are generally getting along very wel we lost a man out of our Co day before yesterday   his name was Abraham Merical he died very unexpectedly   he had bin in the hospital 2 weeks but was thought to be getting along very wel   his brother died the 1st one in the Co   Mat Mount is stil pretty poorly but mending some   we are haveing very stil Christmas   the boys are all in camp   some of the officers is out in the country on a tight   I received your letter and cases a few days ago but as I had just rote I thought I wouldent write for a day or so   I hant had a letter from Anderson lately   we are have very warm nice weather lately   it is just cool enough to freeze a little of nights   there is no furlows granted yet   I dont know whether there wil be or not   I would like to be there to take Christmas with you but as I cant I wil have to be content with writing to you I dont know of anything more to write at present so I wil quit for the present and write some to Cass
I remain your husband and friend as ever
Wm Coffin To R L Coffin

this is rather homely paper to write a letter on but it is all the kind I can get   we cant by hardly anything here now but our Sutler wil have on some things pretty soon

Giles County   Tenn
Dec the 31st 1863

Dear Wife
I this evening take my seat to write you a few lines in answer to your letter of the 18th which I received a day gone by   I was glad to hear that you had got wel again   hope this wil find you and the children wel   I am wel at present   the rest of the boys are about as comon   we have had very warm weath-

er lately til this evening   it has blowed up very cold and seems like some of the changes in Iowa   wel tomorrow is new years and you wanted my new years gift but I dont know what I can send you   there is no stores here that we can by any thing at   I have bin makeing a pipe that I guess I wil send to you so you can se some of my work I allowed to make you a silver ring but I couldent get the tools to make it with   if I get the chance I wil make it yet I got a letter from O C Macy last evening   he is mending   he said the women of mound city made them a free dinner on Christmas   there was 450 sic in that hospital   that was severel to feed   that is the way for people at home to do if they would all do that way they neadent to be afraid of being called copperheads and traitors   every boddy have plenty of chances to proove their lovalty if they wil make use of them   one year ago tonight we camped on the battlefield of Parkers crossroads with dead men laying all around us but we war so tired we dident care much for any thing   tonight our situation is quite different we are in good comfortable houses plenty to eat & C   yet the main thing to make a man happy is lacking yet but I hope another year wil bring that around   that is the presence of our homes and familys I think one more year wil send the traitors howling to their holes and liberate the old Stars and Stripes and the old American Eagle   the emblem of the best government in the world and the Pride of all honest men so they can soar in triumph over a united America and may the dirty rag that bears the lone star the palmetto tree and the slimy snake the emblem of tyrants and traitors go where Wards duck went never to be heard of again   this Jan the 1st 1864   it is the coldest this morning we have seen since we came to Dixey   the frost is flying like Iowa I wil bring my letter to a close

I remain your affectionate husband as ever

William Coffin To Rachel L Coffin

Jan the 10th 64

Dear Wife

I wil try to write you a few lines I am wel as common the boys are generally wel Weir Couch is very sick he was taken day before yesterday very sudent and very severe he went to the hospital yesterday he has something like the pneumonia we have had pretty cool weather for 3 or 4 days the ground is bare-ly coverd with snow the first we have had this winter the veteran troops are passing nearly dayly going home on furrows and to recruit the 7th Iowa went along on the 7th Jess Williams has gone in again if you wil go up and se him he can tell you something about how we are getting along what kind of a place we are in how soldiering goes & C I was on picket when they passed here and he was in a hurry so I dident get to talk to him but a minute I would have sent you $5.00 by him if I had thought of it before he was gone I sent you $5.00 in the last letter I sent you I want you to write whether you get it or not write

whether you got the $40.00 I sent you fromCorinth Krysher is the fatest I ever saw him he stand it very wel since we come here Mat Mount ant very stout yet but he is stil on the mend I wil quit for the present write often
I remain your affectionate husband
Wm Coffin to R L Coffin

Jan the 18th 1864

Dear wife   I
now take my pen to write you a few lines I am wel as common and hope this wil find you and the childre wel I received your letter of the 3rd last evening it is the first letter I have had for two weeks I was glad to hear that you stil keep well Weir is mending slowly but not able to get up any yet the rest of the boys are all doing very wel we stil have some pretty rough weather it is snowing some tonight and looks as though it might get to be pretty stormy you neadent to be uneasy about meenlisting unless the whole Regt would go in and they wont do that I dont propose to go in any mor til I get through this term some of the boys have got a letter from Dallas stating that Wil frank and Julyann had got back if old Luse gets back I want to sel out there, I was 29 years old yesterday I waid 180 lbs that i14 lbs more than I ever waid in Iowa tel henryI think I am big enough to woller him yet I would like to take a skuffle with them again and se who would come out best tel Sis I would love to hear her sing some tel her I want her to be a good girl and help mother all she can and learn her book so she can spell and read for papa when he comes home I want you to learn them all you can I dont know of any thing more to write at present so I wil quit writ often
I remain your affectionate husband
Wm Coffin To R L Coffin

Fort pull tight   Murray Co Tenn
Jan the 22nd 1864

Dear wife   I this evening take my pen to write you a few lines I am wel as comon and hope this may find you welWeir is getting along very wel he thinks he wil be able tocome to the Co in a few days I hant had a letter from yousince I wrote before we hant had any mail for 3 days we have bin mooveing since I wrote we mooved yesterday weare about 9 miles north of where we war we are guarding some trusel work on the rail road there is no other Co here there is two companys below here and the rest are above here scattered along the railroad there is tolerable good quarters here though not quite as good as we left but we can fix them in a few days so they wil do very wel it is a tolerable nice place here and we have a splendid spring rite close there is a meeting house in

78

3 hundred yeards of here and they are going to have meetings there next Sunday I hant bin at meeting only in camp since I left home but I am going a Sunday I nothing happens it is a citizen that is going to preach this is a union settlement rite around us all that I have seen of the neighbors seem very friendly and willing to accomadate us all they can   we have a very snug little fort here that would take severed rebs to get us out of this is a very broken country we cant go any where with out climbing either up hill or down our camp is rite on a hill side I saw the completest piece of machinery last evening I have seen in Dixey it is a machine to gin, card and spin cotton all at the same time they put the cotton in with the seed in it and turn a cranck and it comes out thread it spins 6 threads at a time dont know of any thing more at present so I wil close write often

I stil remain your affectionate husband

Wm Coffin To R L Coffin

Maury Co Tenn
Jan the 28th 1864

Dear wife   I this evening take my pen to write you a few lines though I dont know that I have any thing of much interest to communicate only that I am wel and I hope this wil find you and the children wel it has bin so long since I heard from you that I begin to be afraid there is something the matter the last letter I got was wrote on the 3rd it had the last haff dollars worth of stamps in it the boys are generally wel all able to be with the co except Weir he was mending when I heard from him last we have had very nice weather for a week or more the citizens are begining to plow some, I went to meeting last Sunday and heard a very good sermon from a young man that had bin in the rebel army a year but he seen the errors of his ways and turned from them as all good men should do our Chaplain preaches here next Sunday the people here nearly all belong to meeting from what I can learn it seems the most like a Christian land of any place we have bin in since we left home I like being out by our selves much better than to be where there is more troops we have bin working on our stockade for 3 days and it wil take a half day yet then we wont have any thing to do only get our wood and go on guard about twice a week we have got our quarters fixed very comfortable I like this place to take very thing together the best of any place we have bin at since we have bin out got a letter from Anderson last evening he said he would get the money for the corn and wheat in a few days and send it to you he has spent $25 that he had but says he wil get it if I want it I guess I wont hurry him unless you are likely to get out when you write tel me how much you have on hand I want you to buy your own flour and meat &C and pay up as you go and if you want bed clothes or any thing of the kind and ean buy them do so and it wil be all right as far as I am Concerned if you could buy stuff and make some new bed clothes it would be a good thing

I wil close for the present write often
I stil remain your husband as ever
Wm Coffin to R L Coffin

write whether you got the $5 I sent you or not

Sunday evening
Jan the 31st 1864

Dear Wife   I this evening take my pen to write you a few lines   I am wel as comon at present the boys are generally wel I received your letersof the 10th & 16th evening before last I was glad to hear that you was wel we stil have very pleasant weather Old Peter preached to day there was quite a turn out from the country it seems the most like a civilized land here of any place we have bin in got the envelop you sent but I dont know any thing about it I never sent I sent you a letter about the time that was mailed with $5 in it that ant my hand write and I always back my own letters I dont know what to make of it want you to write whether you got the $5 or not I got the stamps you sent we can get stamps and paper here now so you neadent to send any more   you seemed to think I mite get a furlow to go home but there ant any chance I hant heard of any getting furlows only them that has reinlisted I guess if you was down here you wouldent think that v half of the soldiers are at home we cant hardly miss what is gone the cars hant got to running here yet but I guess they wil in a week or so this feb the 1st all wel we had quite a storm last night it rained very hard for a while. I got a letter from CFldwell last evening he said there was two lambs come in the cold weather about Christmas and both lived and are doing wel he says the old sheep loo very wel I dont expect we could have left the sheep at a better place, I dont know of any thing more at present so I wil close we are going to have a big mess of eggs for breakfast I wish you could help eat them with me eggs are only worth 20 cts per doz tel henry I want to know which was the bigest him or his grand pop when they war sleighridin   I expect he felt the bigest I would like to there to be there to slayride with you some but I expect I would nearly freeze after being use to a warm climate so long I wil close for this time write often
I remain your husband as ever
William Coffin To Rachel L Coffin

I got a letter today that weir had got from Anderson he writes that he had sent you $55.00 by express he sent me an amount of everything I guess he is keeping things very strait if you get the money and wont kneed all of it you may let father have what you have to spare I want to pay him for the timber as soon as I can there is no writing between us if you pay him any he can give you a receipt for it and it wil be all right I want you to keep plenty and write to me how much you have to spare you had better keep enough to do you 2 or 3 month for I dont know when we Wit be paid off again I shad send you as much as $10 a month all the time Weir Couch has come to the co again wil send you a gold pen in this

Maury Co Tenn
Feb the 5th 1864

Dear Wife

I this evening take my pen to write you a few lines I am as comon the boys are generally wel I received your letter of the 21 of last month 2 days ago I was glad to hear that you and the children stil kept wel there is no news of any importance here the weather ant quite as nice as it was awhile back we had an old man from Polk co with us last night he lives close to kryshers folks he says Rachel is so fat that he dont think one bed cord would hold her and Wes is fatter than you ever saw him I was weighed the

other day I weighed 180 lbs I want you to write how much you weigh I want to know whether it agrees with you or not to live by your self I believe it agrees with me very wel but I dont like it atall I went a fishing yesterday with a pin hook I Matched enough for my breakfast I think I wil have all the fish I want from this on I wish if you can get hold of 4 or 5 small hooks you would send them to me we cant get any here I cant get my likeness taken now there is no body about here that takes pictures if the cars get to runing maybe some one wil come in if they do I wil have mine taken and send it to you I dont think I look much older than I did when I left I guess I am tanned a little blacker than I use to Weir got a letter from Meshack Couch the other day they write that they have got in their own house they say they have a good warm house Anderson wrote that he had sent you $55.00 I wrote to you about it in my last letter I sent you a gold pen I want you to write whether you get it or not, I want you to pay father what money you have to spare I want to pay him for the timeber as soon as I can I want you to keep all you kneed for your own use I wil close for the present

I stil remain your ever wel wishing husband

Wm Coffin To R L Coffin

Maury Co Tenn
Feb the 11th

Dear Wife   I this evening take my pen to write you a few lines in answer to your letter of the 28th of last mo which I rec last evening and was glad to hear that you and the children was wel I am wel at present and hope this wil find all wel the boys are generally wel we have had very nice weather lately the citizens are begining to plow rite smart Cap Marsh is gone home on a leave of absence D Russel is commanding the co he is a bully fellow we have a fine time while Cap is gone we are expecting to be paid off again pretty soon I guess you had better keep the honey and use it your self as it wil be a heap of trouble for Jess to fetch it and very uncertain about me getting to se him and I guess you had better send the locks by mail you can send any thing that dont weigh over 2 lbs by mail for 8 cts and that is better than to bother any body with them if you send them by mail tap them up wel and put one paper on the in side of the locks with the directions on it so if the out side gets tore off the other wil be good I think you had better lay in flour enough to do you til after harvest if you have any money to spare when you get that from Anderson pay it to father I wrote to you about it once but thought maybe you wouldent get it I wil close for the present for my candle is nearly out and I hant any more and our mail goes out very early in the morning
I remain your wife affectionately
Wm Coffin To R L Coffin &C

Feb the 15th 1864

Dear Wife I this evening take my pen to write you a few lines I am wel as comon at present and hope this wil find you and the children wel I received your letter of the 4th last evening and was truly glad to hear that you and the children was stil wel Anderson wrote to me that he had sent you $55 by express I supposed he had wrote to you to let you know when to go after it but I recon he dident think it necessary he aimed to do things up right I guess but he hant a much of a head for business I got a letter from Anderson last evening they war all wel Will Frank Davenport and his mother are haveing a law suit about the little black colt old Susan is chargeing him for takeing care of him when he went home sick from the Army and takeing care of Suce a year ago big business for mother and son I hope they wil leave that country before I go back there I never want to live amongst such folks they are worse than heathens there was 4 Co of the old 2nd Iowa went on to pulaski yesterday I am glad to hear of the soldiers drilling them copperheads a little if they wil give them enough of it they may take a likeing to it and enlist and be soldiers I dont know of anything more to write at present so I wil close

Feb the 23rd 1864

Dear Wife I this evening take my pen to write you a few lines though I dont know that I have anything to write that wil be likely to interest you I am wel at present and hope this wit find you all wel I hant had a letter from you for a week but hope to get one the next mail the cars have got to runingthey have made 3 trips they wont run but every other day for awhile we have bin have-ing some very nice weather lately we got a letter from Anderson today they war all wel old suse Davenport and John Z are talking of moveing to Pella Wil Frank and Suce lives with old Johny Ro Frakes has bought old Ant Ably out and is going to build and moove on his place, John kings father in law bought little George Davises place and is going to build up on the state road George bought Macys place and they bought over on the quaker ridge that is all the changes I have heard of Lute Davis has got home from the peak he fetched his wife with him Dave Clark is feeding for Haste Hill for 75cts a day a poor low lifed dog used to swear he was better than any damd negro but now doing what the most the negroes in this country want do they want be waiter boys for any secesh no they shoulder their guns and fight for liberty and right and proove themselves to be honorable men to the side of them poor pesky sneeking lowlifed cowardly traitors at home that are so fraid that a negro wil be their equals if they dont want to be the equal of a negro they ought to try to occupy a higher position that that of a negro when he was in bondage I got a letter from O C Macy last evening he is getting about wel thinks he wil be with the Co soon

      Joel Couch wants to move in to our house I dident like the idea mutch but wrote if he has a mind to obligate himself to leave whenever I wanted him to that he mite moove in I have bin makeing some rings for you and the children have made one apiece for you they ant very nice but I thought as I hadent any chance to send you any thing nicer I would send them the least one is for sis and the black one for henry and the other for you as I have nothing of importance to write I wil close
I remain your affectionate husband as ever
Wm Coffin To R L C

Murry Co Tenn
March the 5th 1864

Dear Wife I now take my pen to write you a few lines. I am wel at present & hope this wil find you and the children wel the boys are all wel I received your letter of the 13th of last month this evening I was very glad to hear from you and to hear that you was all wel it had bin two weeks since I had got a letter from you before I guess your letters all come through but some of them are a good while comeing, this is election day Tenn is going to try to establish civil law again and live under the old stars & stripes I was up at Cobioca today and seen unkle Jonathan Rolls he is stil unwel but able to be up the most of the time it is likely he wil be discharged soon Sunday after dinner and all wel we had preaching at eleven oclock there was a good turnout and good attention paid to a good sermon how I wish for the time to come when we can go to meeting together and enjoy one anothers company as we use to but we wil stil wait and maybe time wil bring all things right after awhile we have very nice weather now, the cars have got to makeing a trip every day we hant had much male for about a week I wil have it fixed all right about the money that Anderson has spent weir wil pay me some here and I want Anderson to have some rails made and hauled out to tighten up the fence which wil take some I am a going to send you a present in this this the 7th and I wil finish this I received your letter of the 23 this evening I was glad to hear that you was all as near wel as you was I hope the children wont have the hooping caugh bad I hant rec but 3 letters from you wrote in last month one wrote the 5 one the 13th and one

March 7 & 8, 64

Cap Marsh got back here tonight he says he liked to have froze to death while he was at home he is fat and hearty   he got 7 new recruits for our co they wit be here in a few days Cap fetched a letter from Joel they are all wed Old Suse has sold out to little C Teorge Davis bully I say Wes got a letter stating that Rachel had the Dipthera but not bad tel granny that I am sorrow to hear that she was so unwed I hope she wit be better soon you seem to think if I was there you could take some of the fat off of me maybe you could I dont know but I would be very willing to risk it a little while for I could spare a little verry well I hope that you wit be able to get along til I get home if you get a little poor I think I can soon fatten you when I get home   I guess I have wrote enough of that kind Cap says that 6 companys of the 7th Iowa have gone down the rest are at nashville I dident se them that went down I dont know whether Jess Williams has gone down or not I would be very glad to se him, it is late bed time and I wit quit for the present
I remain your loveing husband as ever
Wm Coffin To R. L. Coffin

after breakfast the 8th

we had quite a storm last night our shantys leak some the one I live in is just about such a thing as our old house was but it dont leak quite as bad I am keeping nouse now there is 8 of us in together and we take it 3 days around washing dishes cooking meet &C we have cooks to bake our bread and make coffee but we cook our other things we had some tree mollasses for breakfast I wish you could have had some I am going to get 2 old hens today and have a pot pie I wish you could help eat for I know it wil be good I wil quit this wil go out this morning Yours & C

(no date - Approx. March 15, 1864)

Wel Leuzenah   I wil write a few lines to you though I have wrote about all that I can think of at present to father Since I was writing to him I have bin up through town this is a farelly good sized town the houses are generally large have bin owned by rich old secesh it has clouded up again and is pretty cool we are burning rails almost without number I was very sorry to hear of you and the children being so unwel I you wil get along without getting any worse hant had a letter from you since the one you wrote the 23rd of feb the mail dont seem to come as it ought to to the regt I guess we wil stay here a few days and maybe a good while we cant tel Jess said henry sent me an apple but it got so mellow it mashed before he got here he give me a tin cup full of butter which was very exceptable I wil close for the present write often and let me know how you and the children gets along
I remain your affectionate husband as ever
Wm Coffin

Athens Alabama
March the 23rd 1864

Dear wife
I now take my pen to write you a few lines in answer to your letter of the 13th and 15th which I rec last evening I was glad to hear that you and the children was getting along as wel as you was I hope the children wil get over the hooping cough before they take the mumps I want you to be as careful with them as you can and maybe they wont have the mumps very bad I am wel as comon at present the boys are generally wel we have had pretty cool weather ever since we come here night before last it snowed about 2 inches deep more by half than had bin before this winter it nearly all went off yesterday but it is pretty cool yet it looked a little odd to se snow 2 inches deep and the peach trees

and garden flowers out in bloom we are building quarters here we are putting up log houses 16 by 20 feet square I dont know whether we wil get to stay here long or not we wil have the most of them up by the last of this week we are liveing in rail pens which answers a very good purpose when we cant do any better we got a letter from Anderson a few days ago they have lost their baby the rest of them war wel frakeses got their house burnt and nearly everything that was in it there was no boddy at home but the children Joel Couch has mooved in Andersons old cabbin and wont go in our house you neadent to be uneasy about me enlisting again for I think if I serve 3 years that wil be my share if all do that much I think the rebelion wil be put down I would rather have bin at home all the time if Icould have done my duty and stayed there but I felt it my duty to come it wasent because I thought I would like soldiering better than liveing at home tel granny that I would like to have her likeness very wel if I could take care of it but as it is I guess she had better not send it if she is amind to have it taken and let you keep it til I get home I would be very glad to have it I am sorrow to hear of her haveing the hooping cough for I know it is very hard on her we got 5 new recruits for our Co a few days ago and 2 more are comeing that we know of I think it is about time that some of our venerable connection were doing something for their country if they ever intend to do any thing I have wrote about all I can think of at present so I wil close write often

I remain your affectionate husband as ever

Wm Coffin To Rachel L Coffin

Athens Alabama
March 28th 1864

Dear wife   I

now take my pen to write you a few lines I am wel at present and hope when this reaches you it wil find you and the children wel the boys are generally wel we have had some tolerable pleasant weather lately though cool for this season of the year this far south it is raining today and the wind is very high and cold the regiment have all got in to their houses some of them ant quite done yet but wil be in another day or so we have the nicest quarters we ever had and we put them up the quickest they are built of round chesnut logs 16 by 20 feet square we put up and finished off about 5 houses a day on an average I received a letter on the 26th from you that was wrote on the 14th of Feb it had bin nearly 6 weeks on the road it was directed plain enough but from some occasion it took it a long time to come through John Jenkins of our Co died at Mound City Illinois lately he hant bin with us since we left Corinth O.C. Macy is about to be transfered to the Invalid Corps if he is he wil never be with the Co any more. Sam Goodwin stayed here last friday night he was on his way up to prospect to his regt to se the boys he belongs to the pioneer corps yes-

terday was easter Sunday but we dident have any eggs eggs are scarce here and
sel pretty high we cant get things here like we could at graces trestles with the
exception of that this is a very good place our duty is light we only come on
guard about once a week the water is good and plenty here our camp is close
to a nice little creek and we have a good spring to get water out of to use I
would be very willing to stay here a while since we have got good houses up
and are getting so wel fixed the citizens ant making much arrangements for
farming around here they have all bin rich old cubs and had their negroes to
work for them now their negroes are all gone and they dont think they can work
at all but by the time they starve a year I think they wil be willing to dig for
their own liveing tel henry I would like to have some of his eggs I think I could
eat a good many of them for him tel Sis I want to know whether she has got so
she can help her mother much yet or not I seen severel little girls 6 & 7 years
old up in Tenn that could card and spin cotton rite along I wil close for the present write often
I remain your busband as ever
Wm Coffin To R L Coffin

Athens Alabama
March the 31st 1864

My Dear wife
                                                                              I
this morning take my pen to write you a few lines to let you know how I am
getting along I am as wel as comon and I hope when this reaches you it wil
find you and the children wel I received your letter of the 20th last evening and
was glad to hear that you was wel I hant had any letter from Dallas since I
wrote to you before we have got our houses all done we are building cook-
sheds now after we get that done we wil build the officers quarters the let us
build ours first we have generally had to build theirs first we got 12 new
recruits to the Regt last evening we got one to our Co the weather is stil cool
here it froze a little last night we have orders to drill 4 hours a day from this
on but I guess it wil play out pretty Soon I hant heard of Jess Williams being
a going to go home to recruit I dont think it is so I would like to have them
socks if you have them on hand yet you can send them by mail it only takes 8
cents to send any thing under 2 lbs to a soldier if you send them lap them up
wed so the paper that the directions are on wont get tore off there is some comes
sometimes with the paper tore off til they cant tel who they are for tel Henry
that if I get a chance I wil make him a ring that wil fit him I wil give you the
prices of some things here eggs is worth 25 cts per doz butter 60 cts lb apples
5 cts apiece and other things in proportion tel granny I would like to se her and
have a good chat with her I am glad to hear that she is getting better of her
cough Sam Goodwin was talking when he was here the other evening that he

would as leave se granny as any of the young folks I wil close for the present
I remain your affectionate husband as ever
Wm Coffin to R. L. Coffin

(Note: This letter is apparently missing the first part. The date is also in question. written sometime between

April 01, 1864 & April 15, 1864

to return to our familys and friends once more   we have had rather rough
weather the most of the time since we came here yesterday and the day before
war about the only nice warm days we have had since we come here   it has
bin raining the most of the time today   we are drilling 4 hours each day and
the new recruits 6   wel mother I would have bin very glad to have had a little
bit I had have knew I could have got it   I would have sent for some   we
cant get any thing here without paying 2 or 3 prices butter here is 60 cts a lb
and so strong it out ranks our Colonel   I wil quit and write a few lines to
Jeremiah   write often
Wm Coffin

Wel Jeremiah I wil try to write a few lines in answer to his letter which I rec
yesterday   I got the fish hooks but wont get to use them while we stay here
there is a few little fish in a little creek lose here but none large enough for the
hooks he sent   I wil keep them and maybe we wil get to some larger stream
he wanted to know what I thought about him going in to the Army   I dont
know that I am capable of advising any body but I would advise him to stay at
home I dont think he can stand soldiering wel very wel   I think there is plenty that is more able to soldier.   I was to go a hundred times I would go in and
old Regt every time   it ant half as hard on a new recruit if they are with old
soldiers that knows how to take care of themselves and have officers and
Doctors that know their business   if any of you go in to the service I would
be very glad for you to come here if it suited you   I wil quit for this time
write when convenient
I remain his affectionate brother as ever
Wm Coffin To Jeremiah Coffin

brother James Jones as I have bin writing to nearly all the rest I wil finish by
writirg you a few lines   you wanted to know how I liked the climate.   I can
tel you I like the climate very wel but I dont like the country atall   where it is
level it is generally poor soil and not healthy   the water poor & C   the people through here also in Mississippi look as though they had bin fed on custard

& rice all their lives   up where we war in tenn the soil is rich the climate nice the water good but the hills are so steep that a coon couldent hardly clime them and a great portion of the land to rocky to plow at all   if you have a notion of the South I believe my advice would be to take a trip

Athens   Alabama
April the 15th 1864

Dear wife

I this morning take my pen to write you a few lines I am wel as comon at present, and I hope this wil find you and the children wel I received your letter that was wrote the 4th & 6th this morning I was very glad to hear from you but I am sorrow to hear of you haveing such a sore throat but I hope it wil be better before you get this I want you to take as good care of yourself as you can am glad to hear of the children getting along so wel with the mumps and whooping cough I was afraid they would have a hard time I hant had any letter from Dalles since I wrote before there ant much of anything going on about here of importance there is a few prisners fetched in every few days there was ten fetched in yesterday there is a good many reffugees comeing in from south of the Penn river they say that union people cant live down there any more there was 10 or 12 familys come in last night they look pretty pitiful they have to leave everything they have and get away the best they can our Regiment is relieved from picket duty and put to doing Provest duty that is guarding prisners store & C around town we are drilling 4 hours a day now there is some of the reverent genuine southern aristocracy here I saw a very fine lady the other day out takeing a pleasure walk with her little poodle dog in her arms and she was steping so short that a fellow couldent have drove a flax seed in her ass with a sledge hammer they consider it a disgrace to be catched carrying their babys but if they carry a little dog they are all right we hant had very much warm weather yet this spring it has bin cool and rainy the most of the time since we come here tel Granny I am sorrw to hear of her haveing such poor health but I hope she will get better soon I would be very glad to se her and talk with her again better soon I would be very glad to se her and talk with her again tel henry I dont want him to get to sassy to other folks tel them I would send them something if I had any thing to send but I hant and I have no chance much to get any thing   as I have nothing of interest to write I wil close write often

I remain your husband affectionately

Wm Coffin To R L Coffin

Athens   Alabama
April the 20th 1864

Dear wife   I this evening take my pen to write you a few lines though I have nothing of importance to write   I am wel as comon at present and hope this may find you and the children enjoying the same good health I hant had a letter from you since I wrote before I am very anxious to hear from you as you wasent wel when you wrote before I am always anxious to get letters from you but when I hear that you or the children are sick it makes me more so, we have had very pleasant weather lately but stil rather cool it frosts nearly every night I hant had any word from Dallas since I wrote before Weir got a letter a day or so ago they was all wel Weir is mending some but I dont think he wil ever be very stout any more he hant done any duty for 3 months unkle Jonathan Rolls was about so when I seen him last I hant seen him for a week I started my likeness to you a few days ago want you to write and let me know whether it gets through or not and whether you think it looks like me I waid 173 lbs the day I had it taken I had another one taken that I allowed to send to Ruth but if you dont get the one I sent I wil send the other one to you it is just taken on a plate Ruth has bin wanting one ever since I left there I wil close for the present by requesting you to write often
I remain your affectionate husband as ever
Wm Coffin To Rachel Coffin

Athens Alabama
April the 23rd 1864

Dear wife   I this morning take my pen to write you a few lines am wel at present and hope this wil find you and the children wel I received your letter of the 11th and the socks you sent me I was glad to hear that you was as near wel as what you was I hope you wil have good health while I am away for with good health we can stand amost any thing I think the socks are very nice and thee that knite them has and wil be remembered and respected by me under all circumstances though many miles seperate us   we got a letter from Anderson evening before last they war all wel but their Milton boy he had a lung fever and was pretty sick Anderson dident write any thing about that fellow going in to my house he hadent got the letter yet that I wrote to him about it Macys folks are talking of getting their old place back and Nate Mendinghall is talking of buying Tom Bilderbock place north of McClelens Dine wont have a colt this spring I am glad of it as she is young and I expect they wil work her pretty hard Ruth writes that they have meeting there occasionaly and are trying to do better than they have done before I dont know whether they have joined or not I think that settlement is going through a kind of a purge and wil come out better than it was before. I want you to writ in your next letter what you want done with the wool this season it wil soon be sheering time and caldwel wil want to know what to do with it if you want to work it this season I wil order them to send it to you the first opportunity I want you to write how you fixed it about that timber what father aims to charge for it &C we hant bin paid off lately I hope we wont be til there is 4 months due us I would rather they would only pay us every 4 months tel henry that he ant big enough yet to have a gun when he gits big enough to use one I wil get him one tel Sis I am glad to hear that she is learning to sow so wel Cal Hills little girl sent him a silk handkerchief that she had hemed it was very wel done and I think sis can do as wel as she can for I know she is as smart a girl I wish you would send me a handkerchief and if sis can hem it let her do it I would like to se some of her work it is so warm down hare that a person neads a handkerchief in the summer time I want you-to send the children to school all you can tel granny I hant seen Sam Goodwin since I wrote before and likely I wont again soon he is down at Decator in the Pioner Corps we dont have much chance to viset around here some of our boys get to go to Nashville and Huntsville every few days on the cars to guard prisners but I hant got to go either place yet wel I must tel you that I seen a negro woman the other day that had bin a slave til lately that was so near white that her hair was red and strait and her eyes was blue and she was a very good looking woman besides now they may say all they pleze about abolitionist wanting to sleep with negro women & C it may all be so but the fact that there any more than one full blooded African in ten in the south prooves that nobody can beat

the southerners for amalgamating with the negroes I wil close for this time I still remain your ever wel wishing husband and father
Wm Coffin To R L Coffin & children

Athens Alabama
April the 29th 1864

Dear Wife

I this evening take my pen to write you a few lines I am wel at present and hope this wil find you and the children wel we have had very warm weather for a few days with a goodeal of rain we are ordered to be ready to leave this place at 4 oclock tomorrow morning I dont know where we wil strike for probably Dalton Georgia there is no doubt but we are going quite a trip somewhere we only have two teams to the regt and the men carry 3 days rations from the start which makes it look as though there was to be a quick trip made some where there ant to be a tent with the whole force the officers have to carry their

own rations and eat the same as private soldiers do I guess when we all get together there wil be quite a good sized squad of us. I expressed a box of clothing to you this morning there is a blanket and one pair of states belongs to A N Ludington and one over coat belongs to T T Vancleave you can open the box and take out mine and and take care of the others til there is some one passing to Adel that you can send them by safely the blanket and skates are to go to old John Ludington and over coat to TomVancleaves wife there is no hurry about sending them to them wait til there is a good chance I sent you my likeness in my parents packet dident know whether you would get the other one or not so I thought I would send you another one I sent Ruth one that I had taken that wasent a very good -one if you get both of them you can keep them both or let mother have one just as you please Weir wont be able to go on this tripI guess he wil be left here for a while with a good many others that ant able to go on a march one of Co Gs boys married an Alabama girl last evening 12 years old rather tender picking I think it wil hurry him to get enough good of her in a night and one day to pay marriage expenses but maybe he rates it higher than I would some of the boys in Co B tried to kill old Cap Dikeman last evening but war prevented from it by a guard   he ought to have bin killed long ago he uses his men like as though they war dogs we get the pleasure of guarding 11 robbers while they work on our breast works here they cant treat them as prisners of war so they make them earn their grub on the breast works and bunk in the guard house at night this after supper the mail has come and I dident get any letters   I hant had a letter since I wrote before I was in hopes to have got one before we left here the order was red on dress parade for us to start precisely at 6 in the morning the boys that ant able to march and not sick enough to be in the hospital war sent to Nashville this evening Weir went among the rest it is not likely they wil be with the Regiment again soon. I hant heard from Anderson since I wrote before Jane Hill Cals sister was married to George Fish a brother to Mrs. Wineheart while he was at home on a 30 days furlow he belonged to the 2nd Iowa battery and has reenlisted I wil close for the present write often wil write again the first opportunity
I remain your affectionate husband as ever
Wm Coffin To Rachel L Coffin

May the 5th 1864

Dear wife
I this morning take my pen to try to write you a few lines I am wel at present and hope this wil find you all wel   hant had a letter from you for 2 weeks we nant had mail but once since we left Athens but I guess we wil get some today we started from Athens on the 30th of April and marched to Larcansville and took the cars about noon yesterday and landed here about 10 oclock last night we are in about a mile and a half from Chatanooga I guess we wont stay here

longer than today and likely we wil go on today I guess we wil be kept a moove for some time now we have had very pleasant weather for traveling since we started except the first day and night it rained pretty hard we are near the foot of lookout mountain it looks pretty rough it looks as though it would be a hard task to go to the top of it without have an enemy to contend with there is a considerable force here now the cars war runing all night last night bringing in troop it looks as though there would be something done in this direction pretty soon we leave here at 8 this morning so I wil have to bring my letter to a close write often

I remain your affectionate husband as ever

Wm Coffin To R L Coffin

Ringgold Georgia
May the 13 1864

Dear wife

I this morning take my pen to write you a few lines I am wel at present and hope this wil find you all wel we are up here now guarding a wagon train we wil load today and start back tomorrow we war down in snake creek gap about 12 miles nearly south of dalton we war within 5 miles of the railroad runing from Dalton to Atlanta our forces war fortifying when we left we have a very heavy force in there and I wouldent be surprised if there was something done before we get back we are going to whip them at Dalton certain but I cant tel how soon it is a very mountainous country around Dalton which wil make our advance slow our Regiment had a sharp skirmish on the 8th and come out all right they killed 2 and took 2 prisners we have had very nice weather the most of the time since we started out we have marched every day but one more or less but not very hard any of the time I have stood it very wel sofar the boys have generally stood it wel and are in fine spirits our regiment can march equal to that many grayhounds and they are getting tougher every day I wish you would send me $2 in your next letter I lost my pocket book a few days ago with what little change I had and what postage stamps I had I hant had a letter from you since I wrote before we dont get mail very often we cant get mail nor send mail outonly when there is a heavy train passing with a guard you musent be uneasy if you dont get letters very often for when we go back to the command it may be some time before there wil be a chance again to send a letter there is about 300 wagons in our train and that looks as though ought to haul enough hard tack and sow belly to do us some time I wil close for the present

I remain your affectionate husband as ever

Wm Coffin To R L Coffin

May the 19th 1864

Dear wife

I take my pen to write you a few lines   I am wel at present and hope this wil find you all wel   I rec your letter of the 5th last evening   I was glad to hear that you was wel   this is the first time we have had a chance to send mail since we war at ringgold   we have been marching more or less every day since   we are now bettween Rasica and Kingston and wil moove on soon   you can learn more about our movements from the papers than I can tel you   I think we are giveing the rebs fits and if we keep going so a few weeks we wil have them cleaned out   we had quite a scratch with them on the 16th our regt was in front for 3 miles we lost two men killed and 4 wounded in the regt nobody hurt in our Co we are pressing old Johnsons rear very close I dont know where the race wil end   we have bin out 20 days and marched 13 of them   the troops are standing it wel the weather has bin nice the most of the time I got a letter from anderson last evening they war all wel he said there was nobody in our house yet he was thinking of renting it an old widow woman I got the fish hooks you sent me but I dont know whether I wil get time to use them soon or not we hant had time to wash a shirt since we started   we have bin long enough at a place a time or to but dident know we was going to stop long enough   we we got no washing done   I wore one 15 days and put on another I think again I wore it that long I wil have a chance to wash we have to start no more

yours as ever

Wm Coffin

May the 20th 1864

Dear wife

I this evening take my pen to write you a few lines I am wel at present and hope this may find you all wel   I wrote some to you yesterday but we had to moove before I got through writing and as I have a chance today I thought I would write a little more for fear I dont get a chance soon again   we are now camped 3 miles north of Kingston on the railroad the cars have bin runing through here today they have bin runing bridge timber railroad hands & C down below to repair the road ahead   we are laying over here today to wash and clean up a little   I think we wil take atlanta in less than a month if we have no bad luck every thing looks to be working as wel as could be desired   you wanted to know what I thought of the war   I can tel you I think we wil clean them out pretty soon I dont think they can stand 2 months more like the last two weeks has bin   the prisners say that they hant any as strong places as some they have lost   it looks to me as though they had got discouraged and afraid to risk a generel engagement any more   they have georgia South Carolinia and texas troops to cover the retreat   they dont dare to put tennessee Kentucky or any of

their more northern troops in the rear for fear they wil come over to us   what dead and prisners I have seen seem to be pretty wel clothed and their haversacks wel filled with corn bread and meat   their tirds along the road looks like coon tirds in roastenyear time   t here is a goodeal of brand mixed in I wrote to Anderson to send you your part of the wool the first opportunity I want you to keep the children going to school   do all you can to make them like to go and take an interest in their teacher   tel granny I am glad to hear that she is wel I would be very glad to se her once more I stil feel in hope it wont be long til we wil all get to go home we may have to serve our time out but I dont think so at the present   I wil quit for this time and write some to mother I remain your ever wel wishing husband
Wm Coffin To R L Coffin &C

Rome Floyd Co Geo
May the 25th 1864

Dear wife   I this evening take my pen to write you a few lines, I am wel at present and hope this wil find you wel   we came to this place on the 22nd Rome is about 15 miles alittle north of west of Kingston on a branch of the road runing from Dalton to Atlanta the place was taken on the 18th by the 14th Corps after about one hours fighting the enemy retreated leaveing a good lot of salt meal flour camp equipage & C the most of the rich citizens left with the rebels leaving their bedding furniture and house property in generel which the negroes & poor whites appropriated to their own use as fast as they could carry it to their homes they had a heap of good machinery here which they left undamaged a good printing press in order   they left lots of papers half printed all giveing glorious news on their side   I wil send you one of the 10th I dident get one of the latest ones though I seen some and red them   Rome is a very nice town and tolerable wel fortified   they could have held it for some time in spite of us if they had have had the sand in their gizzards to make them fight   there is more farming going on between here and Kingston than any place I have seen before in the south   there is lots of large wheat fields and cornfields they seemed to have bin perfectly confident that they would hold the place this summer we drew flour and meal today we had slapjacks for dinner the first soft bread we have had for 25 days we had a fine shower last evening which put the roads in good order for marching they had got very dusty before the rain I dont know how long we wil stay here maybe severel days we dont get any news from below that we can rely on I red your letter of the 18th of April on the 22nd it had went to some other regt before it come to me we dont get mail here only every 3 or 4 days the road is in runing order but we have plenty of rations that was captured here so they have no nead of runing a train here very often to this place   some of the pork captured here was put up at

Cincinati   they have just now issued 4 big pkgs of tobacco to the man, that was taken here   it is good tobacco such as our sutler sells at $1.00 a plug   I have wrote about all I can think of at present so I wil close for this time
I remain your husband as ever
Wm Coffin To R L Coffin

Rome Georgia
June the 1st 1864

Dear wife
I this morning take my pen to write you a few lines I am wel as comon at present and hope this wil find you all wel   we are haveing tolerable warm weather for a few days past   the prospect at present looks fair for us to stay here some time yet   we war expecting to be relieved by a portion of the 17th Corps but they passed by yesterday going on to the
front   we hear canonading below here this morning   I guess the 17 th Corps has run in to a squad of rebs and are sending them a few compliments   we are fortifying some here   the rebs fortifications here all face one way and we have to build some to defend the other side   it ant likely we wil ever be attacked here with anything but cavalry   we are
camped on the bank of the hightower river about where it and the Oastanauly come together which form the Coosa river   Rome is rite in the forks of the river each river is as large as Scunk River there dont appear to be many fish in them we cant catch any to do any good   in one mile of hear is where Strait was captured with his whole command about a year ago   they war fetched in to town and the women spit in their faces and on their hands and they mad their negroes spit on them they dident think then that the yanks would ever get here   now they are over powered they are as friendly people as I ever saw   sometimes they complain about the boys taking things from them   we tel them to recollect how they served Strait and his men and they dry up in a hurry a great many of the worst rebs left here when their army left   if we stay here 2 or 3 weeks longer we wil begin to live pretty wel vegetables wil begin to do to use and is lots being raised in this country.

This the 2nd and I wil finish my letter   W e are haveing quite a wind storm at present and looks as though we would have rain soon we got mail today I got your letter of the 11th was glad to hear that you war all wel we dont get mail here but about once a week   the cars dont come here very often   we dont get any news from the front to amount to anything I wrote to Anderson about sending the wool to you Levi Davis and Marg McClellen and Jake Vanmeter and several others from about adel have enlisted for 100 days   I want you to write how you are getting along for money if you get out you must borrow to do you til we are paid off which may be some time yet I want you to keep the children under your control as wel as you can and not allow them to be saucy to any body and keep them a going to school and and learn at home all you can I want you to send the deed to the timber up to Anderson and let him have it recorded I hant heard any thing from Wier since he left Athens I have wrote about all that I think of at present so

I wil close for this time remain your affectionate husband

Wm Coffin To R L Coffin

Rome Geo
June the 8th 1864

Dear wife I this morning take my pen to write you a few lines I am wel as comon at present and hope this wil find you and the children wel I rec your letter of the 24th of May a few days ago but as I had just wrote I dident answer it til now   there is nothing of importance going on in the military line about here at present and we cant hear anything from the front lately we are stil digging away here a building breastworks and it wil take some time yet to get don but when we do get them completed it wil take a pretty smart force to get us out of here I got the money and stamps you sent they came in very good play for I had bin borrowing ever since I lost my pocket book and the boys are generally getting scarce we have had a good deal of rain lately which is a good thing on soldiers that are marching it is easyer to march in a little mud than in the dust the prospect looks fair for us to stay here some time though we cant tel any thing about it to any certainty I hant had a letter from Dallas since I wrote before I heard from Weir he is at Pulaski Tenn he is getting stout some of the boys that was with him come on to the regt they say he is fat as a hog and doing wel tel nathan that I want him to take Jin to some good horse if he hant done it I want to keep her busy a raising colts tel granny I would like to se here very wel and I think if we take Richmond and Atlanta before the spring campaign closes we wil be in a fair way to get to go home soon I feel very anxious to go home but I hope before my time is out we can all go home together with a complete victory on our side then it would be some satisfaction to go home and to live there after a person was there I have wrote about all that I can think of at present so I wil quit for this time

I remain your affectionate husband as ever

Wm Coffin To R L Coffin & C

Rome Geo
June the 22nd 1864

My dear wife   I this morning take my pen to write you a few lines   I am wel at present and this wil find you and the children wel   I received your letters last night of the 18th of May and the 8th of June   I was glad to hear that you war wel   hope you wil continue to have good health while I have to be away for I should hate to hear of you being sick.   I want you to get along the best you can, and stay where you can get along the best   I hope it wont be a great while til this war wil be over and we can live together in peace and quiet again   I want you to take as good care of the children as you can   keep them wel clothed and plenty to eat and teach them in the way they should go as near as you can   I now you have a pretty tough time but it cant be helped at present so we must stand the best we can and hope for better days   I rec 50 cts in your letter of the 8th which is the 3 letter I have got with money in   you neadent to send any more   I wil have enough to do me some time   dont know when we wil be paid off though   I think we wil be paid before a great while.   I expect you had better quit sending the children to school as they are pretty young to go any way if they dont like to go it wil be apt to do more harm than good to send them.   I am glad to hear that Jin Colt ant as ornry as you first though it was   for I dont like to raise stock that ant worth any thing after it is raised   I have wrote about all that I can think at present so I wil quit and write some to granny and   father & mother
I remain your affectionate husband as ever
Wm Coffin To Rachel L Coffin

Dear Grandmother
I wil try to write thee a few lines though I dont know that I can write anything that wil be interesting to thee   we are getting along very well here at the present   the are generaly wel   we can get a good many berrys here now which makes our liveing a gooddeal better than it was a while back   the citizens around here are in rather destitute circumstances   a good many are allready drawing provisions from our comissary   we may all be very thankful that our lots wasent cast here in the south   for them that live here see pretty tough times   nothing more though than the most of them deserve   I must close for the present
I remain thy friend as ever
Wm Coffin to grandmother

Rome Geo
June 28th 1864

Dear wife   I now seat myself to write you a few lines   I am wel and hope this wil find you and the children wel   I received your letter of the 13th 14th & 15th of this month   I was glad to hear that you was wel   the boys that was left at Pulaski got here the 25th   they are mostly wel Weir looks tolerable wel we have had some very hot weather for a few days t here is generel hospital established here for the accomodation of 6000 sick and wounded   there is allready severel here and more looked for soon from the front   I rec a letter from Anderson a few days ago they war all wel he says the prospect is not very flattering as a generel thing up there for a crop   Becky Clark was very sick with iresipelas and lung feaver   he dident write whether there was any body in our house or not   I have wrote to know two or 3 times but he dont give me any answer yet   you want to know what I think about you mooveing back there this fall   now I dont se how you could live there through the winter unless you had some one to stay with you for it would be to bad for you to get up and make fires of cold mornings even if you could get the wood choped and carried in besides   besides there would lots of other things that would have to be done that I dont think you could stand in the cold weather   I expect Anderson would get wood or do anything he could but you know how he is always heels over head in work   it seems to me if you could get along where you are til spring and then go up it would be better, but you can use your own judgement and do what you think best   I dont know how tight the house is whether it would be comfortable to winter in or not   when you write tel me how you allowed to work things whether you aimed to get any one to stay with you or not &C   I dont think you could raise much garden w ithout me there to put the ground in order &C   if you could go there in the spring you mite rase a little late garden stuff a few chickens & C   I had bin making calculations some time for you to go back in the spring but I hadent thought of you going sooner   I guess I can send you $70.00 when we are paid off   I want you to send me a few postage stamps we cant get any here   I have bin borrowing ever since I lost mine except what you sent me   I stil thought we could get some or I would have sent sooner   send 3 or 4 in each letter for 3 or 4 of the next letters you write I guess you wil begin to think you have me to support instead of me supporting you but I hope it wil change before long   tel granny I am getting along very wel except laziness   it is about all I can do to hold my eyes open this hot weather ant as fat as I was   I lost 20 lbs on the march from Athens here and have gained about 5 back again I weigh 165 lbs now I have wrote all of interest at present so I wil close
I remain your loveing husband as ever
Wm Coffin To R. L. Coffin

Wel Mother I wil write a few lines to thee   I hant made any inquiry about
Indigo seed yet   I wil though the first chance I have I have never heard any-
thing said about whether it growes here or not I wil quit for this time write
often with love
I remain thy affectionate son
Wm Coffin To Mother

Rome Geo
Sunday evening July the 3rd 1864

Dear Wife   I this evening take my pen to write you a few lines to let you know
how I am getting along   I am wel at present & I hope when this reaches you
it wil find you all wel   we have bin haveing some very warm weather lately
we are haveing a very nice shower at the present which I hope wil cool the air
some   I hant had a letter from you since I wrote before   I got one from
Anderson this evening wrote the 20th of June he wrote that it was stil very dry
up there   the wheat and oats was heading out not higher than the stubble ought
to be he said there R was lots of corn not come up yet from all accounts there
wont be a very heavy crop in that part this year   he says Joel has 10 acres on
our place that is about 3/4 of a stand and Anderson has 10 acres that he planted late and plowed it in   that he says is a tolerable good stand   I am in hopes
there wil be enough raised on the place to pay the taxes if no more he says he
dont know of any chance he wil have to send your wool to you but wil send it
if there is any chance   we had preaching in camp this evening for the first
time since we come here   we wil have a generel review tomorrow   is about
all that we wil do to celebrate the 4th I wish it was so I could spend the 4th with
you and the children but as it ant at the present we wil have to be content with
things as they are. there is stil some sick and wounded fetched here nearly
every day there is about 1400 here now mostly sick Jess Williams and Newton
are both here Jess come on the 27th of June and Newton on the 1st of July
they are neither one much sick   Newt is able to do some work as waiter or
nurse Jess is able to be up and about but pretty weak with the diarea   we have
heard of the death of 4 of the boys that was wounded in our regt I wrote to
you in my last letter to send me some stamps but for fear you dont get it I wil
write it again   we cant get any here atoll I have put off sending thinking that
we could get some til I have borrowed a bout a dozen and got none to pay with
I have wrote enough for the present so I wil close
I remain your affectionate husband as ever
Wm Coffin To R L Coffin

Rome   Geo
July the 11th 1864

Dear wife   I this evening take my pen to write you a few lines   received your letter of the 27th of June this evening   was glad to hear that you stil keep wel. I am in good health   at   present   the boys are generally wel   we stil have very warm weather   we are liveing tolerable wel now   we can get all the black-berrys we want which helps out considerable   we get very good bakers bread to.   wel you wanted me to promise you that I wouldent enlist any more   I can promise you this much   I shal   serve   the time out that I have allready enlisted for first and then take a furlow to suit myself and talk to you about it before I go in again   I dont know what would be best about you moveing to your self   it dont look to me like you could stand it to winter up on the farm unless you had somebody to live with you it looks to me if you could get a house close to your fathers or mine one it would be better then if you froze out you could have a place to go to   it looks to me as though it would be best for you to try and get along down where you are til spring though you can do what you think best   there is no talk yet of us being paid off soon I guess we wont be paid til the campaign is over and the troops settled again   you must keep the children under as good control as you can   I am wel aware that you have a hard time with them and a poor chance to learn them to behave them selves   you must recollect old Jobe and take pattern from him by being patient in all things I dont know whether there wil be any furlows given this summer or not   they ant giveing any yet only to sick and wounded   if there is any chance I shall try to get one.   I wil send some plumb seed in this I sent some in my last   the small ones are a very nice little plum   they are different from any I ever saw   the large ones are a big blue plum nearly as large as a guinea egg.   I want you to take good care of them I have wrote about all at present so I wil close.
I remain your affectionate husband as ever
Wm Coffin To R L Coffin

Rome Geo
July the 20th 1864

Dear wife   I this evening take my pen to write you a few lines   I am wel at present and hope this wil find you all wel   I received your letter mailed the 6th last evening   I was glad to hear from you but sorrow to hear of sis being sick but hope she wil be wel by the time you get this   we are stil haveing very warm weather but not so warm for a few days past as it was for some time before   I received the handkerchief you sent me I think it is very nice and   I hope to be able to do as mutch for you sometime   I got a letter from Anderson last evening they war all wel he says the bugs is nearly ruining the wheat   it wasent far enough along to tel whether they would take it all or not   there is no one liveing in our house O. C. Macy is at home on a furlow   he ant very stout yet   for the want of something to write I wil close for the present

I remain your affectionate husband

Wm Coffin To Rachel L Coffin

July the 25th 1864

Dear wife   I this morning take my pen to write you a few lines in answer to your letter of the 13th which I rec evening before last   I am wel at present and hope this wil find you all wel   am glad to hear that the children have had the measels and got over them.   I got a letter from Anderson wrote the 14th   they war all wel   Anderson says the kitchen of our house can be made warm by pasting paper over it.   I guess it was seiled with rough timber and the joints are a little open. Anderson says he wil get your wood and do your milling but I dont want you to depend to much on them for you know it is uncertain about you and them getting along very wel   I would rather you wouldent moove up unless you could get some one to live with you that could help you about make-ing fires & C   if you can get Dick or one of the girls to live with you, I think you might get along but unless you could get some of them to live with you I would rather you wouldent under take it til spring   I have wrote to Anderson to know as near as he can guess about how much wheat and corn we wil have on the place   how the spring is & C   I want you to stil write and tel me what you think of doing about it   I got some stamps the day I got them you sent   I have enough to do me a while   you neadent to be uneasy about me reenlisting while there is so many at home that hant bin out atall   I want all to have a chance to do something for their country so I shant put myself in the way of them that hant bin out yet   I want them to have room when there is an invi-tation write and tel me what has become of Bill Shelly   I hant heard from him for a long time O. C. Macy is stil at home   got his furlow renewed on the 14th for 20 days longer   I have wrote about all of importance at present and some that ant of much importance so I wil close

I remain your affectionate husband as ever

Wm Coffin To R L Coffin

Rome Georgia
Sunday evening   July the 31st 1864

Dear wife   I now take my pen to write you a few lines   I am wel at present and hope this may find you and the children wel.   our Regt is in good health   as a generel thing.   there is severel got the sore eyes is about the worst   Zeak Davis and Cowyer that use to be about McClelens so much about the time we enlisted war both captured the day before yesterday by the rebs   we war out a forageing   we had went out the day before about 25 miles and loaded and stayed all night.   the cavalry had a skirmish in the morning but there was no boddy hurt.   we started then for camp and got back within 12 miles of Rome and stoped to rest and the 2 boys went on about 2 miles and war taken.   they war riding horses that we had captured. Cowyers horse was killed in the road was the only thing to show that they had bin taken   it is supposed that they war guerrillers and would kill the boys as soon as they got them away a little but they may not   our men burnt severel fine houses around there   that is the only way that we can manage them is to make the rich mens property pay for the guerrilla depradations   we are signing the pay rolls today we wil be paid off in a day or so   I dont know how we wil manage to send our money home there is no express line this far down yet   we have had a fine rain today which I hope wil make it a little cooler for a while this is August the 1st and I wil finish my letter   I hant had a letter from you since I wrote   we hant had any mail for 3 days but I guess we wil get some today   it is warm and cloudy this morning and looks as though we would have more rain   I hant had any news from Dallas since I wrote to you before   I have wrote about all that I can think of at present so I wil close
I remain your affectionate husband as ever
Wm Coffin to Rachel coffin

August the 1st   in the evening

I dident get my letter to the office in time for it to go out this morning so I thought I would write a little more   I received your letter of the 23rd of July this morning   was glad to hear that you and the children was wel   you must do what you think best about going up home this fall I dont think you had best go unless you can get some one to stay with you that can make fires & chop a little wood & C   Anderson says he would cut and haul your wood you mite get a long if you could get one of your sisters to live with you if you cant get some of your folks I think you had better stay where you are til spring though you can use your own judgement about it   I got the handkerchief you sent also the stamps you neadent to send any more unless I write for you to   we wil be paid 6 months pay tomorrow $84 as we get $16 a month

from the 1st of may   I dont know of any chance I wil have to send mine home only in letters   I wil close for this time   yours & C
Wm Coffin To R L Coffin

Rome Georgia
August the 6th 1864

Dear wife   I this evening take my pen to write you a few lines   I am wel at present and hope this may find you and the children wel   we are haveing a goodeal of rain lately   it has bin raining the most of the day today and look as though it wouldent stop soon   we got paid off the other day   we got $84 we hant got any way fixed out yet to send our money home yet   our chaplain is likely to get permit to go to Nashville   if he does he wil take our money there and express it   I let Jess Williams and Newton and Jesse Charles have $5 apiece and they wil order their fathers to pay it to father   so you can get it when there is any passing up there   I wil write and let you know when I start the other home so you wil know when to go after it   krysher & I are liveing together cooking our own grub and eating it   we live pretty wel the most of the time   we have plenty of fruit to make pies of and we get plenty of pota- toes and rostenears and if you had have bin here about supper time yesterday evening you could have had the chance of helping eat a yellow leged chicken and a pot full of dumplings   we are both splendid cooks and get everything up according to order.   I wil send the children a present of one dollar apiece in this   I would like to buy them a nice present and send them but there is no chance to get any thing here   so I wil send them the money and let them buy what they please with it.   I would like to se them and you the best in the world but it seems as though that time dont seem to come but I hope after the election this fall there wil be something done that wil bring about peace on honorable terms I have had no letter from you or from Dallas since I wrote before   I wrote Anderson to not send your wool down there even if he has a chance   I thought it would be so late   if you got it now you couldent get much of it worked up before cold weather.   I want you to write as soon as you came to a conclusion about where you wil winter this winter.   I dont want you to undertake anything that wil cause you to be exposed to the bad weather much for you know you cant stand it to be out in the cold & rain   I have wrote all that is necessary at present   so I wil close
I remain your husband as ever
Wm Coffin

Rome Geo
August the 9th 1864

Dear wife   I this evening take my pen to write you a few lines in answer to your letter of the 31st of last month & 1st of this which I received last evening I was glad to hear that you and the children war stil wel I hant got the letter yet that you said you dident date. I have only got two that had stamps in them one had 7 and the one I got last night had 3 in it   I sent the children one dollar apiece in my last letter   I want you to write whether you get it or not.   I let old Peter T Russell have $60 to express to you and I let Jess & Newton Williams & Jesse Charles have five dollars apiece that their fathers wil pay to father at Pleasant Plain   I sent their notes up to him in a letter yesterday I want you to pay father $15 or $20 more on that timber   Just what he thinks is right. you pay him.   I want it settled and then I believe I wil be out of debt once   I dont know what would be best to do with the colt I would like to keep it if it wont cost to much to get it wintered   I guess you had better se what you can get some one of them up there to winter it for and if it dont cost to much get them to keep it   I got a letter from Ruth last evening they war all wel she dident write any thing about the crop on the place   she says dines colt is fat and growing fast she says dine is poor but that is nothing more than I expeeted   our bees hant swarmed yet this year David Clark is very low with typhoid fever and iresipelas she says Milt Hill is haveing a good time with his boys   he has wheat on the old woman kryshers land and corn on Peaboddys so they get in his before they do in what is on my place I am glad he has got it so arranged   he wil se the necesity of keeping them up I am in hopes   I wrote to them to not send your wool down I thought by the time you would get it it would be to late for you to do much with it   tel sis she must be a good girl and help her mother wash her dishes.   tel Henry I want him to send me word whether he is a good boy to carry stove wood and help his moth-er like he use to or whether he has got lazy and a bad boy   tel them I want them to be good children and mind what their mother tells them   I wil close for this time
I remain your husband affectionately
Wm Coffin To R L Coffin

this is the 10th and I wil write a few more lines   it is cooler this morning that it has bin for some time I was out to the field hospital yesterday evening and seen Jesse Hocket Tom Hockets son he is sick   also Elias Mills old Johny Williamses wifes brother he is wounded   we have commenced on our last year   yesterday made 2 years for the most of our Company I wil close for this time write often

I remain your affectionate husband as ever
William Coffin To Rachel L Coffin

Rome Geo
August 12th 1864

Dear wife   I now take my pen to write you a few lines in answer to your letter of the 5th which give the sad news of Henry being so sick I do hope that before this reaches you he wil be better   I shall be very uneasy til I hear again I am wel at present   the other boys are about as comon   I have had no news from Dallas since I wrote before Dr. Wood our 1st surgeon is at home   in Fairfield   Old Peter Russell dident start to Nashville when we expected him to and he ant gone yet   he is waiting for the Chaplain of the 57th Ills to get ready to go with him   we have had more or less rain nearly every day for some time   it is raining very hard now.   as I have nothing of importance to write I wil close for this time write often
I remain your affectionate husband as ever
Wm Coffin To Rachel L Coffin

Cartersville   Georgia
August 22nd   1864

Dear wife   I this morning take my seat to write you a few lines.   I am wel at present and hope this may find you all wel   hant had a letter from you since the one you wrote the 5th   we left Rome on the 15th we only had about 2 hours notice so I had no chance to write before we started we first went to Realcca and laid around there 3 days and then started back to Rome and got within 7 mi of there and war ordered down here   we have bin runing around considerable but it hant amounted to much   old wheeler has bin tareing up the road in diferent places is the cause of us haveing to come out   dont know when we wil get back to Rome but I hope pretty soon   we hant had any mail since we left there   we sent a man back last night to forward our mail but trains run so unregular to Rome that there is no telling when he wil get back as I have a very poor chance   to write I wil close for the present
I remain your affectionate husband as ever
Wm Coffin To Rachel L Coffin

Cleaveland   East Tenn
August the 29th 1864

Dear wife   I this morning take my pen to write you a few lines   I am wel and I hope this wil find you all wel   we have had no mail   since I wrote before we have bin out where there war no chance   to   get mail   I wil give you a description of our trip when I get time   we look to get back to Rome   in a few days but we cant tel   I am so uneasy about Henry that   I dont know hardly how   to   stand   it   til we get to where we can get our mail   this is the nicest town I have seen in the south   their are organizeing the 1st georgia Regt for the union army   here it is   pretty near   full now   I   wil   have to close for   this time   there is a train comeing   that I expect we   wil   go on
I remain your husband as ever
William Coffin To Rachel Coffin

Stevenson Alabama
August the 31st 1864

Dear wife   I this morning take my pen to write you a few lines to let you know where I am & C   I am wel at present and hope this wil find you all wel   we hant had any mail yet since we left rome   we have bin going so fast that our mail hant over took us yet.   I wil try to give you a description of our travels we left Rome on the evening of the 15th   went to Kingston got Supper and started for Resacca at dark got to Resacca at one oclock in the night 16th   laid at Resacca 17th marched out to spring place 11 miles where old Wheeler was said to be fortifying   got there he was gone   we killed 33 head of sheep and was fixing to have a little mutton for supper when we got orders to go back   we started at dark and got to Resacca at one at night 18th   laid at Resacca til in the evening &   took   the cars for Rome   got in 7 miles of Rome &   was ordered back to Cartersville   got there a little before daylight   the 19th we laid at Cartersville   20 we started on a march down the Etawa River   went out 7 miles before breakfast   got breakfast and was ordered back 21   we laid at Cartersville til midnight and took the cars 22   stil going 23 at daybreak found us between Charleston and Riceville where old wheeler had tore up the road (this in east Tenn) here we started a foot towards Knoxville   marched 17 miles and camped 4 miles east of Athens 24th   marched 4 miles and stoped til in the evening marched back two miles and camped 25th   marched 4 miles to Athens and camped 26   marched back to Riceville to take the cars 27th   we got on the cars in the evening we thought for Rome (but a mistake) when we got in 2

12 miles of cleaveland an engine to the train in front of us give out so we had to get off and march in to Cleaveland   28 took the cars in the afternoon and got to Chatanooga before dark and camped   29th got on the cars and come here.   I see I have lost a day some where for this is the 31st but no diference I have give you the rounds   I dont know how long we wil stay here   East Tenn is the best country I have seen in the south   the people are mostly loyal they war recruiting very lively along the road at different places.   I think it is uncertain when we wil get back to Rome   if we ever do hope we wil get where we can get some clean clothes before long   we only fetched what we have on our backs and our gum blankets   if we ever get in shooting distance of old Wheeler we wil try to make him pay for the trouble he is putting us to but I guess it is uncertain about us getting a chance at him   we hant got to se a reb yet since we started   I think it has bin the calculation for our cavalry to drive them on to us but they have failed to do it yet   I wil close for this time for I ant in very good ketter for writing   I want you to write often and maybe we wil get stopped long enough after awhile for our mail to over take us   I am very anxious to hear from you again

I remain your affectionate husband as eve

Wm Coffin To Rachel Coffin

Athens Alabama
Sept the 7th 1864

Dear Wife   I again take my seat to write you a few lines to let you know that I am stil wel   I hope this wil find you all wel   we hant had any mail yet since we have bin out and I guess we wont til we get back to Rome and it is uncertain when that wil be   I wrote to you on the 31st of August and give you a description of our travels up to that time and now I wil tel you where he have bin since then   we left Stevenson Ala on the 1st of September on the cars and landed at Murfeys borough Tenn about 12 oclock that night   the 2nd we started to Lavernge at 2 in the morning and got there for breakfast a distance of 15 miles   staid there til dark and marched back 5 miles and camped in 3 miles of some of the rebs   the third we marched out to a little town called Jefferson expecting to get a fight but the rebs run   the 4th we got on the cars and went out 6 miles south of Murfeys borough to guard some hands that was fixing the road where the rebs tore it up   the 5th we got on the cars in the evening went back to Stevenson Ala got there at midnight and moved out on this road   rode all day the 5th and all night and this morning found us at pulaski tenn   we got our breakfast and shoved out down the road again   we have unloaded here and marched out close to our old quarters and stacked arms   the talk is that we wil march out to Browns ferry on the Tenn River to try to keep old Wheeler from crossing   it is believed that he is trying to get out and wil do it or be captured soon   we have a heavy cavalry force after him   I have wrote more than I expect you can read so I wil quit for this time I have to write with a pencil on my knee a sitting on a rail

write often

I remain your affectionate husband as ever

Wm Coffin to Rachel L Coffin

Rome   Sept 22nd 1864

Dear wife   I this morning take my pen to write you a few lines to let you know that I am wel   I hope this wil find you and the children wel I received yours of the 8th and was glad to hear that you was all wel again we have had considerable of rain for 2 days past.   I guess the rebs have give up fighting us here though they stil lurk around in a few miles of here   there is no talk of us leaving here yet   hope we wil get to winter here   Milton Hill took Calvins hogs up and turned them over to the constable to be sold and Calvins father in law made him give him an order to get the hogs so Milt had the cost all to pay and the constable charged him all the law would allow him   served him right he would let his hogs bother me but as soon as anybody elses got to bothering him he was for putting the law in force but he got beat at his own game and I am glad of it   I guess the crop on our place is tolerable safe for Milt is farming Peaboddys and the old lady Kryshers places so his hogs wil get in his crop before they do in hours   O C Macy hant got back to the Co yet he was at St. Louis the last we heard from him   A N Ludington' David Hiltebrand and Robert Harison started home day before yesterday on furlow   they war all nearly blind with the sore eyes   there is no chance offered yet for wel men to get furlows   I dont mutch look for any chance this fall   I wil close for this time

I remain your affectionatehusband as ever

William Coffin To Rachel L Coffin

Saturday   Sept the 24th

Dear wife   I this evening take my pen to write you a few lines in answer to your letter of the 15th which I received last evening was glad to hear that you war all wel.   I am wel as comon and hope this wil find you and the children stil enjoying the same great blessing. I hant had any news from Dallas since I wrote to you before   we have had a good share of rain for the last 4 days but it has cleared off at last and is tolerable cool   I dont think we wil be apt to have mutch more very warm weather down here this season tel Henry that I would like to se him stepping around in his new boots   tel him to be a good boy and help his mother all he can.   Tel sis I want her to be a good girl   I want you to lay in flour enough to do you for some time and get your winters

clothing and write to me whether you have any money left   if you kneed any
more money I can get it for you if you wil let me know that you kneed it   I
wrote to Nathan to sel the colt if he could get all he thought it was worth   if
not to keep it   I thought he would have a better chance to sel it than you or
anybody else and would know as near what it ought to bring   I wish if you
can get the yarn you would knit me 2 pair of socks and send them to me the
socks we draw ant mutch account to march in   I wore the black ones that you
sent me out on the march last spring and the spotted ones on this last trip   a
good pair of socks wont last more than 20 days to march in   if you knit me
some send them by mail   if you cant get the wool handy I can get along without them   Jesse Charles is gone home on a furlow   if you would go up and
se him he could tel you about what kind of a place we are in here   I have wrote
all that I can think of at present so I wil bring my letter to a close
I am your affectionate husband as ever
Wm Coffin To Rachel Coffin

Rome Georgia
Oct the 14th 1864

Dear wife   I again after a long delay take my pen to write you a few lines
I suppose you have heard long before this that the road was tore up til we
couldent get or send mail   we got mail yesterday for the first since the 25th
of Sept   I got your letters of the 24th of last and the 1st of this month   I was
glad to hear that you stil keep wel   I was unwel awhile back but I am getting
pretty stout again.   Our Regt was in a very hard fight at Alatoona on the 5th of
this month   our loss was very heavy   our Regt went in to the fight with 276
men and come out with 113   out of 10 officers we had 4 killed Lieutenant
Colonel Redfield Lieut Ayss Co A   Lieut Blodget Co B   Lieut Wright Co E
war killed   Capt William bennet and Lieut Crawford war taken prisners
Lieut Russel Co C was wounded   the Regt lost 36 killed 59 wounded and
76 prisners   our co lost   H J Tarr killed O D Russel wounded in the
side slightly Samuel Warford through the jaws severe but wil get wel if he has
good luck   Robert Talbeys leg amputated not likely to get wel Cal Hill in the
hip   William Elder in side of the face Thomas Bell in the knee J J Wright sen-
ior in the elbow J J Wright Jr in the face   C M Graham in the hip and hand
W A Louis in the side   they wil all get wel if they have good luck   Mat
Mount John Hathaway & JohnOsler war taken prisner   it was said to be as
desperate a fight as ever was known   our force was 2208   the rebs 8000   the
fight commenced at daylight and lasted til 4 in the evening when they left
badly whiped   our Regt lost their colors but they done it honorably   Co K
and Co G was put out with the colors to hold a certain place with orders to stay
there til they had orders to fall back and when the rebs got to pressing them
the generel started 3 different couriers to tel them to fall back but they war all

shot before they got there so they got no orders and they held their place til
they war nearly all taken and killed together   Co K had one man to get out
and Co G & the color bearers held on to the colors til the rebels bayoneted
them   it is said that troops war never known to fight better than they did on
both sides   wasent able to go with the regt so I wasent in it   our division
went out yesterday about 12 miles and had a little fight but the rebs dident
stand very wel   there was none of our regt hurt   we had a rite sharp little
fight day before yesterday in a mile of town but our regt wasent in it   old
Hood is working back north and Sherman following him   he wants to get him
as far north as possible then he wil take him in   I hant had a letter from
Anderson since I wrote to you before I heard from the draft in dallas co wil give
the names of what you are acquainted with first on the list isJeremiah Mills
John loper Henry Harper Jim Jones unkle Jonathan Rolls is drafted and Nate
Mendinghall and severel others over on the quaker divide but I guess you dident
know any of them   I guess you had better sel the colt if you can get a good
price for it   I did think I would rather keep it but it wil take a goodeal to fix
up in the spring and I guess it would be best to sel it   I am going to write
anderson to keep what grain was raised this season and to try and have a few
hogs to let you have   make a few rails and haul out and haul some wood & C
I have wrote all I can think of at present so I wil close write often and dont be
uneasy if you dont get letters from me very often for the rebels keep the road
tore up nearly all the time   I wil write when ever there is a chance to send
letters out   I heard a while ago that they had tore up the road up about Dalton
again I look for a gooddeal of hard fighting in the next 3 or 4 week   I think
Sherman wil demolish Hoods whole Army before he gets back again
I wil close for this time
I remain your husband as ever
William Coffin To R L C

Rome Geo
Oct the 27th 1864

Dear Wife   I this evening take my pen for the purpose of writing you a few
lines   I am wel at present and hope this wil find you and the children wel   I
hant had a letter from you since I wrote before the road ant open yet and we
wont have mutch mail til it is   I guess it wil be finished in a day or two   it
is causeing us to have to live pretty rough   we hant had any soft bread for
about 3 weeks they are feeding us on hard tack and poor beef coffee beans rice
and sugar is about the amount of our liveing and wil be til the road is finished
there is considerable talk of us leaveing here pretty soon but I dont know
whether we wil or not   I would be very glad to get to stay here this winter
we have got very good quarters here to winter in   if we could get to stay here
this winter we could get along then til our time is out without building any more

good quarters   I dont know which way we wil be likely to go if we do leave our wounded boys are getting along very wel   they wil all get furlows as soon as they are able to go home.   the weather has bin fine for the last 2 weeks   it has bin cool and frosted nearly every night til last night   it rained and is warm and cloudy today   I wil send some pine seed in this letter   I want to send enough home this fall to start a little pine grove   you can let your fathers folks have some if they want them   I have nothing of interest to write so I wil close for this time   write often

I remain your affectionate husband as ever

William Coffin To Rachel L Coffin

Rome Geo
Oct the 31st 1864

Dear wife   I this evening take my pen to write you a few lines to let you know that I am wel at present   I hope when this reaches you it wil find you and the children wel   our wounded boys are getting along very wel   Thomas Beall had his leg taken off a few days ago   he is getting along very wel. there is stil talk of us leaveing here   I think we are pretty certain to go somewhere but I dont know where   it is generally believed that we wit go to Americus Georgia and likely from there to Savanah   I think we wil get to se the coast before we stop long any where   we have signed the pay rolls today and I guess we wil get 2 months pay in a day or so   some of the Dallas Co drafted men have got this far into Dixey   Jim Jones is the only one that you are acquainted with   I saw him today he looks about like he use to   Milt Hill is drafted   I dont know what Regiment he is assinged to the drafted men dont get to go where they please   Jim is in the second Iowa   we dont get any in our regt   they are putting them in regts that has over a year to serve   Jesse Hocket started home a few days ago on a furlow   he said he would stop and se you and tel you how we are getting along down here.   I wil send you a ring in this Jess Williams made it and made me a present of it for you so I wil now make you a present of it   I have had no news in the way of letters from Anderson or you since I wrote before   we dont get mail very regular   the road is open now but from some occasion the mail dont come very regular   I wish you would send me a few postage stamps again   I am about out and there is no chance to buy any here now and I am afraid there wont be before we leave here   I have wrote about all that I can think of at present so I wil bring my letter to a close   I wil write again before we leave here and let you know when we start & C

I remain your husband as ever

William Coffin To Rachel L Coffin

Rome Geo
Nov 3rd 1864

Dear wife   I this morning take my pen to write you a few lines I am wel at present and hope this wil find you and the children wel   we are stil making arrangements to leave here   they are shipping every thing away from here I guess this place wil be evacated and burnt   I think we wil leave tomorrow though we have no special orders yet   our sick and wounded are leaveing today   we have had no mail in severel days   the trains have run clear through regular but they fetch us no mail   we have no assurance where we wil go to   we have had very rainy weather for two days past but I hope it wil be over by the time we have to start I dont expect I wil have a chance to write any more before we leave and likely we wont have a chance to send mail for some time afterwards so if you dont get any letters for a while you must not be uneasy for I hope we wil turn up all right somewhere   I want you to write often and the letters wil come to us when we stop if not before   I wil send Henry a little neck tie in this   it ant worth mutch but maybe it wil plese him a little I hant got any thing to send to sis   I wish I had but I cant get any thing here I have wrote about all that I can think at present so I wil conclude by signing myself
your affectionate husband
William Coffin To Rachel Coffin

Rome Geo
Nov 4th 1864

Dear Wife   I this morning take my seat to write you a few lines   we war paid off this morning   we got to months pay and settled up our last years clothing account   I lacked $11 takeing up what we are allowed and I got the money for that which made $43 I got   I wil put $35 in this letter and let O D Russell mail it to you when he gets up in Iowa   he is going home on a leave of absence on account of his wound   we have no set time yet to leave here but I think we wil start before long   some think we wont start til after the election   every thing seems to be about ready for to moove   we dont find out yet which way we are to go nor how far   the weather has bin cool and cloudy with considerable rain for severel days as I have nothing of importance to write and in some hurry besides   I wil close for this time
I remain your husband as ever
William Coffin To Rachel Coffin

we dont stil get any mail

Rome Geo
Nov the 9th 1864

Dear wife   I this morning take my pen to write you a few lines I am wel as comon at present and hope this may find you all wel we are stil in Rome and not as much talk of mooveing as there was when I wrote before   I think that the program has bin changed and I wouldent be surprised if we dont leave here for some time though there is no telling   we have had no mail since I wrote before   I would be glad if we are a going to leave here to get off pretty soon and maybe we would get to where we could get mail more regular and get something more to eat   we are liveing pretty rough and have bin for about a month   we get plenty sutch as it is but it consists of hard tack poor beef coffee sugar rice and beans   we have had no flour nor pork or bacon for near a month so you may guess we are getting pretty tired of beef and hard tack yesterday was election day everything went off quiet here   our Regiment polled 268 votes 234 for Old Abe and 34 for little Mack   our Co dident give Mclellen any one   today leaves me just 9 months to serve yet   I long for the time to come when we can go home but I hope by the time our time is out the war wil be over so we can go home and stay there in peace. we war paid 2 months pay and I sent you $35 by mail in a letter   O D Russel was going home and let him take the letter   he said he would mail it when he got up there in Iowa   I want you to write whether it come through right or not   I want you to write whether the colt is sold or not   if you have the money to spare pay father what is comeing to him on the timber and you had better keep enough to do you til toward spring for we may not be paid off any more soon   I wil send the children 20 cnts apiece in this letter I have nothing else to send them so I wil send them a little money and let them buy what they please with it   I have wrote about all I can think of at present so I wil close for this time
I remain your affectionate husband
William Coffin To Rachel L Coffin

in Camp 10 miles south west of Savanna
near Gulf Railroad Geo
Dec 14 1864

Dear wife   I seize the present being the first opportunity for some time to write you a few lines to let you know where we are and how we are getting along & C   I am wel and hearty so is the rest of the boys   we left Rome on the 10th of nov and marched pretty studdy til the 10th of this month   we have had no very hard fighting yet   we run on to them near hear 4 days ago   they seem to be wel fortified   our artilery has bin working on them some   the

114

infantry hant done much yet   we have got them in a shape that we can begin to do something pretty soon   I have seen some things since I left rome that I had never seen before   we have seen the palm leaf a growing regular sugar cane and rice   we are in the rice swamps now   there is no soil in this country it is all sand   we traveled through a tolerable good country for about 250 miles   since then it has bin very ornry   it is the levelest country through here I ever saw   there has bin no hills to amount to any thing since we left Atlanta I was over to the 15th Iowa a little while ago to se   Milt hill and   Nate Mendinghall   Milt has had the measels on the trip   he ant very wel yet   he looks very natural   Nate has stood the trip pretty wel but he has the diarea pretty bad now   I wrote to you at Rome on the ninth and told you I dident know when we would leave   I thought we would have some notice but on the tenth we got orders at 2 oclock to be ready to march in an hour so I hadent time to write   I thought then I would write before I got to atlanta and let you know that we war gone and first thing we knowed they war tearing up the road in our rear and there was no chance to send mail at all   the last letter I got from you was wrote the 12th of October   I am getting very anxious to hear from you again   guess we wil get mail in two or 3 days   they think we can send mail out tomorrow   I thought I would write a letter and have it ready   I wil close for this time   I dont expect you can read what I have wrote
I remain your husband affectionately
William Coffin To Rachel Coffin

Saturday Dec the 17th 1864

Dear wife   I this evening take my pen to write you a few lines to let you know that I am stil alive and wel and I hope when this reaches you it wil find you and the children wel   we got mail this morning for the first time since we left Rome   I got 3 letters from you   one wrote Nov the 3rd   one the 14th & one the 20   I was glad to hear that you and the children war wel   I got one letter from Anderson   they war wel   we are about 10 miles south west of Savanah near the gulf railroad   the rebs and us are tolerable close neighbors our lines are from 300 to 600 yards apart they keep up a studdy fireing on the skirmish line but there ant mutch damage dun on our side   I dont know how it is on theirs there is a creek between us so we cant cross over to them   our Co war on the skirmish line day before yesterday   we war about 350 yards from them   I shot about 35 times at them   I dont know whether I hit any of them or not   that war what I shot for   they shot pretty close to us but dident hit any of us   we mooved camp yesterday and had orders to fix quarters that we can stay in 10 days or 2 weeks   we are in a very nice place for this season of the year   I think it would be very unhealthy in the summer   we are in the rice swamps where the water would be bad in warm weather   I wrote to you 3 days ago and told you that I had no chance to write often   we war

ordered away from Rome   til we got here we had a tolerable pleasant trip though we had some very hard marching we had a few bad days though though the weather was fine the most of the time   I stood the trip very wel   I more sweet potatoes than I ever eat in the same length of time before I never saw the like of them there was on the road   the whole army had all they wanted all the way through and then there was lots left in some places   I dont think one hundred thousand bushels would cover the pile the Army eat on the trip there was corn   plenty to feed the teems and I expect we got here with 10,000 head of cattle   more than we started with   we are liveing a little rough at present   our rations that we started with is out and we hant got any from the coast yet   we look for the wagon train tonight and then we wil have   we only get corn meal and beef at the present   there was 8 of Co K that was taken prisner at Aalatoona got away and come in a few days ago   they said the boys war doing pretty wel   Zeke Davis and A H H Cowger war with them the boys cut a hole through the car and jumped out while they war runing you wrote that Jesse Hocket told you that I said I wouldent go home on a fur-low if I could get one   asI guess he was mistaken   I dont think I ever said anything of the kind I have always aimed to take a furlow if I could get one but dont have any idea there wil be many furlows granted til next summer   you seem to think it would be best to not have Anderson to buy anything til you go up there   I think it wil be best to have him to put up some meat any way if nothing more for fear it cant be bought in the spring   I wil let Joel get up some wood and make some rails for there wont be any body want to do it after it gets hot weather   I wil write to him to not buy a cow til you get up there   dont think there wil be much trouble in hireing somebody to moove you up in the spring   it wil cost you a goodeal I expect but I think you had better try and moove up in the spring   I wil send you a head of rice so you can se how it looks before it is thrashed I have wrote about all I can think of at present so I wil bring my letter to a close
I remain your affectionate husband
Wm Coffin To Rachel

Savanah Geo
Jan 1st 1865

Dear wife   I this evening take my pen to write you a few lines I am wel at present and hope when this reaches you it wil find you and the children wel   I hant received any letters from you since I wrote before   we are haveing some pretty cool weather for this climate   the ground has froze some for two nights past   we have got up tolerable comfortable quarters   we have got fire places to them   we thought at first we couldent get much that would do to lay brick with but we found a place that we got some that would   Nate Mendinghal and William Mendinghall was over to se me today Nate took dinner with us   we

had a long chat   they seem to stand it pretty wel so far   Ethen West is in the 16th Iowa but I hant seen him yet   Nate says Anderson is getting along tolerable wel he says he keeps dine looking tolerable wel   he says she is a good mare   Tom Macy is married to old man Kings daughter that bought little george Davis out   I hant heard where Weir is yet the mail hant got to runing with any regularity yet   govenor Stone of Iowa paid us a short visit today   he seems to take a heap of interest in the soldiers of Iowa   Gen Grant was in Savanah a few days ago but I dident get to se him   I think a part of Shermans army wil moove again soon   it is generally thought that the 15th corps wil be left here   I expect that we wil have a little easzer time if we stay here but the most of the boys would rather go ahead and help give old south Carolina a turn we all want south Carolina to feel the effects of war before peace is made so the she wil know how to appreciate peace when it comes   I dont think there wil be a grezy spot left where old billys boys goes after they cross the Savanah river   we are getting plenty to eat now and our duty is light so we are getting along pretty wel   I have seen fresh oysters in the shell but I hant had any mes yet   it ant but 3 or 4 miles to where they get plenty out of the river   we mustered for pay yesterday   there is 4 mo pay due us now   I dont know as we wil be paid soon   there was a little blockade runner come in here a few evenings ago loaded with sugar tea coffee and peper they dident know that we held the place til they anchored here   they hoisted our colors as they come by our fleet and come in a skooting as Krysher use to say   they thought they war cutting a hog in the ass but when they found the yanks ready to receive their vesel and load I guess they dident feel quite so wel though of course they couldent refuse to let us have it   it is a rite new vesel built here last summer I have wrote about all I can think of at present so I wil quit for this time write often and let me know stil what you think about going up home in the spring
I remain your affectionate husband as ever
W Coffin To R L Coffin
Dear Grand Mother   as I have bin writing to Luzenah and have some paper left I wil try to write a few lines to thee though I dont know of anything to write that would be likely to interest theeI am in good health and gaining in flesh some   I got tolerable poor while we war at Rome   I think if we stay here this winter and we get plenty to eat that I wil get fat again   I think we wil get plenty of rations from this on while we stay here.   I think this war wil be over in a short time if the South dont behave themselves pretty soon some of them wil get hurt and that badly to for we have got them in a shape that we can go where we plese and they cant help it   our army is in the best health and the best spirits it has bin since the war commenced and we have leaders that the world cant beat.   I hant seen Jess Williams for severel days   he was wel the last I saw him so was Newton   I dont get any letters from unkle Wm any more neither from North coon for the lack of something to write   I wil close
I remain thy affectionate grand son
Wm Coffin To Grand Mother

Savanah Geo
Jan 5th 1865

Dear wife   I this evening take my pen to write you a few lines this leaves me wel and hopeing it may find you and the children enjoying the same good health,   we are haveing very pleasant weather for a few days past.   there is no talk of us leaveing here yet and I think the prospects is favorable for us wintering here   we are building heavy fortifications in closer to the city than the old rebel ones are   wel we had a mess of biscuit this morning for the first since we left rome   we got some block tin and Krysher made us a reflecter that we baked it in   baked nice.   I think they war the best I have et since I left home we made us a lot of plates bread pans wash pan and a big pan to mix bread in we are getting pretty ingenious when we are drove to it   Krysher is our tinner   we had a mess of fresh oysters for supper   we took them out of the shell ourselves,   we can buy them for one dollar a bushel in the shell   I wil give you the prices of a few things in Savanah butter is worth one dollar and fifty Cents per pound   cheese $1.50 rice 25 cts per quart   biscuit $1.00 per doz   small at that   ginger bread $1.00 to $1.25 cts for as mutch as a man can eat   the citizens have bin selling at such prices as they use to in confederate money government is a going to establish prices on every thing and make all sell at them prices which I think wil be a gooddeal lower than the way thing have bin selling.   I was over at the 16th Iowa a few days ago   I saw Ethen west he looks very bad   he is nothing but skin and bones   he is stil going around and doing duty but he dont look as though he was able to set up   I never would have knowed him if some of the other boys hadent have told me that it was him   nat Mendinghall stand it tolerable wel   I hant heard from O C Macy for some time   he was acting ward master in a Hospital the last account we had of him.   we seen an account in the papers of some of our prisners being parolled   John Osler of our Co was on the list   I guess Mat Mount ant parolled or exchanged yet   we dont hear anything more from our wounded boys   I hant heard from Wier yet   we dont get but very little mail yet   I have had no letters from you or anybody else since wrote before.   the mail lines dont seem to be regulated yet   I am getting very anxious to hear from you again I want you to write and let me know whether you think you wil moove up on the place in the spring or not   how you are getting along about money & C   there is not talk of us being paid of yet but I think we wil be paid in the course of a month or so.   I want to send enough to Anderson to pay my tax and for haveing a few rails made and a little wood hauled & C   I want you to write how long you think what you have got wil last you and then I wil know how to make my calculations so as to have plenty   if you moove up and go to keeping house you wil want to get a stove either before you go up there or afterwards   I want you to get a good new one when you do buy   I want you to

good articles of every thing you buy   we have made out with old traps long enough so I dont want to get another supply of the same kind   when you get chickens for a start I want you to get nice shang highs   I think if I live to get home it wil take a big chicken to make me a mess   I dont want any scrub stock on the place,   I wil top it off by telling you to get a good pup before you go up home if you can   you may think I am in a hurry writing about such things but some times it takes a good while for letters to go through and we are always liable at any time to moove so that we cant have a chance to send letters   I missed getting wry sowed on the place this last fall by the road being cut so I couldent send a letter til it was to late.   it is bed time and I have wrote more now than is worth reading so I wil quit for this time
I remain your ever affectionate husband
Wm Coffin To Rachel L Coffin

Savanah Geo
Jan 14 1865

Dear Wife   I this evening take my pen to write you a few lines. I saw Jonathan Williams on the 11th   he said he left you and mother very sick   I feel very uneasy and shal til I hear   I have had no letters from you yet since we come to this place   we dont get but very little mail at all   I got a letter from Anderson yesterday wrote Dec 10th
They war all wel   Weir was wel   the last he had heard from him there is some talk of us leaveing here but it aint known certain whether we wil or not   I am wel at present   the boys are generally wel   as I have nothing of importance to write I wil close for this time
I hope I will get a letter from you soon
I remain your affectionate husband
William Coffin to Rachel L Coffin

Savanah Geo
Jan 18th 1865

Dear Wife   I this evening take my pen to write you a few lines   I am wel at present and hope when this reaches you it wil find you wel   I have not had a letter from you yet since we come here   I feel very uneasy since Jonathan Williams came an told about you and mother being so sick but I hope the next news wil be better   there is talk of us leaveing here soon   probably tomorrow I dont know where we wil go to but it is thought that we wil go to Charleston I think we wil go up land though we dont know   a soldier dont know much about what he is a going to do til he gets orders to do it   I was in hopes to have

got a letter before we left here but it looks very uncertain now and I am afraid it wil be some time after we start before we get mail again   I want you to write often and it wil get to me when we get to where we can get mail and maybe we wont get to where we cant get mail atall   I wil write to you again if we dont get off tomorrow   if we do I wil write on the march if there is any chance to send mail   I have nothing of importance to write so I wil close for this time I remain your affectionate husband as ever
William Coffin To Rachel L Coffin

we have just got orders to be ready to march tomorrow morning at 8 oclock I wil send the children a ring apiece in this letter they are some I mad myself they ant worth mutch but I thought as I had nothing else to send them I would send them the rings they are made out of some kind of composition I would have bin glad to have got a letter from you before we left here but I dont suppose I wil   I hope you wil be wel by the time this reaches you   I wil close for this time
I remain your husband as ever
Wm Coffin To an affectionate Wife

Savannah Geo
Jan 26th 1865

Dear wife   I this morning take my pen to write you a few lines I am wel at present and hope this wil find you all wel   I received of nov the 29th a few days ago   it was 7 weeks comeing hant had any word from Dallas since I wrote to you before   I have wrote to Anderson to sel all the corn but 50 lbs that wil do til after harvest and if there ant enough raised on the place it can be bought for less than $1.00 per bushel you wrote that the colt was poor and couldent be sold for what it is worth   I think as it has bin kept this long you had better keep it and if you moove up to Dallas in the spring take it and Jin with you   we have orders to leave here this morning at 7 oclock   it wouldent be worth while for me to say where we are likely to go to for there is no tellin I dont know whether we are to go by land or water   we have tolerable nice weather now   rather cool to be out   the ground has froze some for two nights past   we hant heard from Wier or the wounded boys that was sent back yet I think if we go to Bufort we wil find some of them there.   I have nothing to write of importance and hant mutch time to write so I wil close   I have wrote what I have wrote on my knee and in a hurry and I dont expect you can read it I want you to write often   dont quit writing because you dont know where we are   direct to the regt and they wil come   I wil write when I have an opportunity which may not be long and it may be some time   no telling I remain your husband affectionately

William Coffin To Rachel L Coffin

near Sisters Ferry Georgia
Feb the 2nd 1865

Dear wife   I this morning take my pen to try to write you a few lines to let you know where we are and how I am getting along   I am wel at present and hope this may find you and the children wel   we are about forty miles above Savannah on the Savanah river   we started on the 26th as I wrote   we was to went out a mile and was ordered back on the 27th   we started again and on the eveing of the 30th we got here   we had to make corduroy bridge about half the way   I dont think any boddy but Sherman could moove an army over such a country for the first 3 days   I dont think we traveled over any road but what we could have got water by digging three feet   we have stoped here only to load our train and we wil moove on in a day or so   likely tomorrow   I hant had any mail from you since I wrote   I got a letter from Anderson the next evening after we left Savannah   they war all wel   nothing else of importance   I was in hopes to have got a letter from you before we left here for it is likely it wil be severel days before we get mail again   we have had nice weather since we have bin out except it has bin rather cool   the ground has froze pretty smart every night til last night.   we are camped in the thick pine timber and burning green pine wood which such a smoke that we cant tel when it is clear or cloudy and pretty hard to tel a white man from a negro   especially if they dont wash pretty often   it ant necessary for me to try to tel where we wil go from here for I dont know   it wil likely be towards Charleston   there is no doubt but it wil be through South Carolina and wherever Shermans army goes in south Carolina there wont be a greezy spot left   the boys are all anxious to leave their mark in that state I dont hardly think we wil have mutch hard fighting to do   I dont think they dare to fight a generel battle with old Billy   I think with him is the safest place a man can be in the Army for he drives every thing ahead of him without mutch fighting   I have nothing of importance to write so I wil close for the present
I remain your husband as ever
William Coffin To Rachel L Coffin

Golds Borough North Carolina
March the 25th 1865

Dear Wife   I this morning take my pen to write you a few lines to let you know that I am stil a live and wel and I hope when this reaches you it wil find you and the children wel   I have had no letters from you since we left Savannah we look for mail now in a day or so   the first train of cars come in here this morning at 4 oclock   we have got no supplies yet but think we wil soon   we have had no chance to send any mail out since we left sisters ferry on the Savannah River   only one day at Fuyetteville one day and I dident have a chance to write that day   we got here last evening it is the talk that we wil get rest here severel days   there was six of our boys that was sent back from Rome got with us last evening among them was Weir and Cal Hill and N Lutington O D Russell is here in town but he hant come to the Co yet   Weir is only midling stout   the rest of the boys are very hearty and stout. Ethen West is dead Nate Mendinghall and Mil Hill are both back sick   as I am on guard today and hant much time to write I wont try to give any account of our camping this time I wil write more when I have more time   I want to hear from you very bad for it has bin so long since I did hear and you wasent wel then makes me quite uneasy. I wil close for this time my pen is very bad and I have a poor place to write   I expect it wil bother you to read what I have wrote but I wil try and do a little better next time
I remain your ever affectionate husband
William Coffin To Rachel L Coffin

Goldsborough   N   C
March 27th 1865

Dear Wife
              I this morning take my pen to write you a few lines this leaves me wel and I hope it may find you and the children enjoying the same good health   we got mail yesterday for the first since we left Savannah   I got 4 letters from you   one wrote Jan the 26"   one feb the 1st   one feb 26 and one March the 1st I was very glad to hear from you but sorry to hear of you and the children not being wel but I hope you wil be by the time this reaches you I also got a letter from Anderson and one from Charley Graham my old bunk mate that was wounded at Alatoona   he is discharged and at home a cripple also one from Sarah West inquiring about Ethen   andersons war tolerable wel there was a goodeal of sickness in the settlement John Longmore died not long since   Anderson said that our place wasent rented yet   he dident know whether he could rent it or not   he hadent sold the corn yet but said he would

if he could get $1. 00 per bushel   he said there was none selling at that yet   you wrote that you dident know of any way of getting up home only to go on the stage   it looks to me as though that would be rather a poor way for you couldent take mutch of anything   it looks to me as though you had better not go than to go and leave your things down there but you may do just as you think best   I dont know how soon we wil be paid off but I think we wil be paid in 2 or 3 weeks   when we are paid we wil get 4 months pay and maybe 6 if you kneed money before I am paid borrow what you want if you can and if you cant write to me and I wil borrow it for you and send it to you   I am going to write to Anderson if he cant rent the place to sow 4 or 5 acres of corn for cow feed.   wel I told you in my last letter that I would give you a description of our trip   we left Sisters ferry on the 5th of feb and struck out through south Carolina   we went pretty direct to Columbia the Capital of the old Rebel state there we had some fighting   we took the place on the 17th and it was burnt that night it was a very nice town and a nice situation   it now stand marked among the things that have bin from there   we went out south east and tore up railroad 2 days   from there we went north east crossed the Waterree River at liberty Hill   went in one mile of Camden where there was hard fighting in the Revolutionary war from there to Cheraw an old town but not very large and thing looked old & wore out   I was in a old church house there that was said to be 103 years old and was used in time of the Revolution for a Hospital   it was a very good house yet   it was small and built old fashioned   there was two graves at one corner that was said to be generel Marions and generel Lumpters though there was no monuments to show who they war   we crossed the great Pedee River   crossed the line between south and north Carolina between Cheraw and Laurrel Hill   from there to fayetteville   there we stayed 2 or 3 days and thought we war going to get supplies up the Cape fear River, but from some occasion we war ordered away from there in a big hurry   I guess it was to help old scofield   we come on til we got in about 20 miles of here   we found the rebs in force fortified   we prepared and give them a good grubbing which made them scratch
gravel   we then coze on here   got here the evening of the 24 of March mak-ing 57 days since we left Savannah making I guess the longest campaign ever known without any supplies only what was started with   we foraged all we could off of the country   we found plenty of corn and meat both salt meat and cattle some sweet potatoes and other things   south Carolina is a very level country and the most of it very poor we had a heap of rain which made the roads bad   I think we corduroyed very near half the road we traveled over on the whole trip   N C as far as we have got is level sandy and the most of it very poor though we saw some very good country when we first got in to the state   we dident use N C as bad as we did south Carolina   we wanted to make south Carolina know how to appreciate peace and plenty if they ever are so lucky as to have such things again   Golds Borough ant mutch of a town though it is a nice situation t he talk is that we wil stay here 3 or 4 weeks   we

are getting plenty of rations and wil get clothing in a day or so   there is lots
of the men got barefooted before we got through   my shoes and clothes lasted me through tolerable wel we are building quarters here that we can stay in a
while   we ant building very extensive   we have built so often that we are
getting tired of it   the weather has bin nice for some time   it frosted last
night and night before which was the first for some time past   I have wrote
about all that I can think of at present so I wil close and write some to father
write often
with love I remain your husband affectionately
William Coffin To Rachel L Coffin

Dear father & Mother as I have bin writing to Luzenah I thought I would write
a few lines to you as it has bin a good while since I had a chance to write to you
or any boddy else   we have just ended a long campaign   I stood the tramps
all right and come out nearly as fat as I started in   the boys generally stood
it wel   we had one man to die in our Regt   we had one wounded and none
killed   when we got through to Fayetteville we had 15,000 loose negroes with
us and could have had 4 times as many if we had have had any way to get them
along that couldent take care of themselves   I have give Luzenah a brief
description of our trip which you wil see   I think when we start on another
campaign we wil go out through Rawly and probably from there to
Greensborough   I want you to write and give me a description of where you
was raised   how far from different towns & C   where Bennys father lives
& C so that if I should get up in there I can find them   I would like to get to
se the country where you was raised   give me the names of as many of the
connection that lives in there as you can   I think when unkle Billy makes
another moove with his western boys old Lee wil come out of Richmond like
as though his shirt tail was a fire   he cant stay there long if we make another
campaign in towards Richmond and destroy the rest of their railroad   the last
campaign deprived them of half the railroad they held 2 months ago   they cant
run any road in S C now and we have nearly half of N C   no the question
is where is the supplies to come from for Lees Army   I have wrote all of
importance at present so I wil close   write when and as often as convenient
I remain your son affectionately
Wm Coffin To Hervey & Rachel Coffin

Goldsboro N C
April 1st 1865

Dear wife   I this evening take my pen to write you a few lines I am wel and hope when this reaches you it may find you and the children wel   I received your letter of Jan 18th a few days ago it was about 10 weeks a comeing   I rec yours of March first   the first mail we had after we got here which is the latest I have had from you   I am very uneasy about you and the children as you war all unwell when you wrote   I hope you wil get stout again and stay so til I can get home to take care of you   I have had no letters from Anderson since I wrote to you before   I dont know whether he has rented the place or not   I think unless you get pretty stout you had better not try to moove this spring and not then unless you can take your things with you   I would be glad for you to moove up home if you and the children was wel and you had a good way of going but you would be likely to have to undergo some hardships and unless you was stout I would rather you wouldent undertake it   but you can just youse your own judgement about it   I wrote to you before about it but thought maybe you wouldent get my letter and I would write again   I wrote to you to borrow money if you get out   I dont know whether we wil be paid off before we leave here or not   there is talk of us being paid off in a short time and there is talk of our leaveing here soon so we dont know whether we wil be paid before we leave here or not   I want you to borrow what money you kneed to use and I wil send you what I can as soon as we are paid   we wil be paid just as soon as we stop long enough at a place to pay us off   I dont know whitch way we wil go from here but it is generally believed we wil go to Weldon   you may listen to hear of something being done in 2 or 3 weeks after Sherman makes another generel moove   we had meeting in camp this after noon   a man by the name of Roach spoke   he belongs to the Sanitary Commission he is from Desmoine Iowa   he issued enough potatoes crout and pickels to all the Iowa soldiers here for one days rations   it was quite a treat as we have been where we couldent get sutch luxuries for a long time we have got some little pole shantys up covered with shelter tents and gum blankets which makes tolerable comfortable quarters for this climate at this season of the year   as I have nothing of importance to write   I wil close for this time I remain your husband affectionately
Wm Coffin To R L Coffin

you wrote to me that you was at your fathers but dont aim to stay long if you got able to go back so I wil direct my letters to Pleasant Plain til you give me diferent orders

This letter is not dated. It is estimated that it was written on April 03, 1865

Dear wife   I have bin writing some to father and wil write a few lines to you though I have nothing of importance to write   I have bin writing so often that I am about runout of anything to write   I was very glad to hear from you and to hear that you war all on the mend   I hope by the time this reaches you it wil find you all wel again.   I would like to be with you all the time but when I hear of you or the children being sick it makes me more anxious to be with you I hope I may not have to hear of you being sick any more til I get home if I should be so fortunate as to get home whitch I hope I wil   I want you to write what your doctor bil is and other expenses by being sick so I wil know what arrangements to make   write to me as soon as you determine whether you wil move up home in the spring or not   corn is worth $1. 00 a bushel and if you dont rnoove up I wil have the most of it sold and I dont know but it wil pay to sel all but about 100 bushels any how   I have not heard yet whether Anderson is likely to get the place rented or not for next season   there is no talk of us being paid off before we leave here and I am glad of it for I think it would be pretty uncertain sending money from here   as I have nothing of importance to write I wil close for this time
I remain your husband affectionately
Wm Coffin To Rachel L Coffin

I wil send Henry some shirt buttons in this

Goldsborough N. C
April 5th 1865

Dear wife   I this morning take my pen to write you a few lines in answer to your letter of March 22" which I rec last evening   I was very glad to hear that you and the children had got wel again for I am always uneasy when I hear that you are not wel. I am wel as common   the boys in the Co are all wel there is nothing certain about us leaveing here yet though there is a goodeal of talk about it   for my part I dont think we wil stay here very long   you wrote that you was agoing to sel the colt if you could I dont want you to do it for from your account of it it wont fetch half what it is worth besides I want some young stock and there is as good a chance to make something out of a poor colt as anything else   I ant afraid but what I can fetch it strait if it lives til I get home and it is wintered now and if it dies let it die mine   I wrote to you when I first came here to borrow money if you kneeded it   if you could and if you

couldent to let me know and for fear you cant borrow what you want I have made arrangements with Jess Williams for you to get $25 of his father he gave me an order which I wil send in this letter if you kneed it go and get it and if you keed any more let me know and I wil se that you have it from some source I can borrow all I want to I dont know whether we wil be paid off before we leave here or not if we ant we wil get the more when we are paid you had better not pay the doctor bil til I am paid off I want you to use all the money you kneed to make you and the children comfortable I dont want you to stint your self because I ant getting paid off I wrote to Anderson from Savannah to sel the corn if he could get $1. 00 a bushel and I dont want him to sel unless he can get that as I have nothing mutch to write I w il close and write some to father and mother
with love I remain your affectionate husband
Wm Coffin To Rachel L Coffin

Goldsboro N. C
April the 9th 1865

my Dear wife I this morning take my pen to write you a few lines I am wel at present and hope that when this reaches you it may find you and the children enjoying good health we are haveing very nice weather of late I hant had any letter from you since I wrote before there is stil talk of us leaveing here soon but I dont know when we wil start the teams are ordered to be loaded ready to start in the morning but I dont know whether we wil start then or not and probably we wont know more than an hour before we start I think there is no doubt but what we wil leave here soon I think our course wil be west or north west through N C probably we wil be guided a goodeal by old Lee I hant had any letter from Anderson since I wrote to you I wrote to him to not sel the corn unless he could get $1.00 per bu. I sent you an order in my last letter to get $25.00 and I want you to get it if you hant borrowed money before if you get it receipt for it and write to me and I wil fix it with Jess if that ant enough to do you til I am paid I want you to borrow all you kneed it may be that we wil be where we cant write for some time if I know you would kneed any more I would make arrangements for you to get it before I leave here but if you do I dont think there wil be any trouble in you getting it Jess Williams said I could have all I wanted so if you cant get what you kneed any where else handyer go to John Williams and I guess you can get it without any trouble, there is 2 1/2 milions dollars sent to pay Shermans Army but we cant get to stay in one place long enough to get it but it wil come good when it does come I wil send you about $90.00 when we are paid I wil get $96 our payrolls are fixed out now for 6 months pay there has bin a great many recruits come to Shermans Army within the last few days tel Henry that I want to know what kind of a dog he has got   whether he is as good as old bounce or not   tel him and sis I want to know whether they have bin going to school or not and how mutch they have learnt & C   our time wil be out in 4 months from today and I hope to live to se that time and get home to enjoy civil life again   we war to have had preaching this forenoon but it was put off til evening to give the boys a chance to wash their clothes ready for the march   I believe it is the first time I have washed on Sunday since I have bin in the service.   I have wrote about all of interest at present so I wil close for this time I wil write again before we leave here if I have a chance   if I dont get to dont be uneasy and dont quit writing   I dont think we wil be cut off from communications as long again as we war before.

I remain your husband as ever
Wm Coffin To Rachel L Coffin

Goldsboro N. C
April 10th 1865

Dear wife   I this morning take my pen to write you a few lines I wrote to you yesterday but I dident know then certain when we would leave here   we have orders this morning to be ready to start at 10 oclock this morning   I dont know yet whatch direction we wil start   our teams are loaded with double their common load   I dont know whether we wil be clear away from communications or not but I think we wil for a while at least   I wil write again the first opportunity but if you dont get any letters for a while you must not be uneasy   you wil be to hear where old Billy Sherman is and we wil be with him   you must bory what money you kneed and take as good of your self as you can   as the mail wil go out in a few minutes I hant time to write any more good by for this time

I remain your husband affectionately
Wm Coffin To Rachel Coffin

Morres ville N. C
April 19th 1865

Dear wife
            I this morning take my pen to write you a few lines   I am wel at present and I hope this may find you enjoying the same   we left Goldsboro on the 10" got to Raliegh on the 14" and come out here on the 15" and have bin laying here ever since this is twelve mi from Raleigh on the railroad   there is none but our division out here of our Corps   the rest are at Raleigh   Gen Logan was out here but mooved his head quarters back to Raleigh this morn-

128

ing the talk is that Johnson has surrendered his whole army but we have no
official notice of it yet   it ant worth while for me to try to give any news for
you wil get all the news through diferent sources before you get this   I think
we wil go back to Raleigh from here   I dont think we wit go any farther west
the railroad is in runing order to here   we feel that our fighting is over and that
we may probably get home yet a little before our time is out.   if it wasent for
the sorrowful news of the assassination of our noble president we could receive
the other news with joy   but as it is it seems like grief and joy mixed   as I
have nothing mutch to write   I wil close
I remain your husband as ever
William Coffin To Rachel Coffin

Near Raleigh N. C.
April 25th 1865

Dear Wife   I this morning take my pen to write you a few lines to let you know
how I am getting along   I am wel at present and hope when this reaches you
it may find you and the children wel   we came back here from Morris ville
on the 21"   we are camped about two miles from town in a nice grove where
we can get good water   I hant had a letter from you since we left Goldsboro
the last I got was wrote on the 21 or 22 of March   I got a letter from Anderson
wrote the 10" of April   he wrote that he had rented ten acres of our place to
Louis Macy to be sowed in wheat and was about to rent 20 to Bill Frank
Davenport for corn   he thought he could rent it all before it was to late   he
said he had sold 30 bushels of corn and had bought 4 pigs for $3.00 apiece   he
said he was going to send you some money in a few days   he says Dine wil
have a colt this spring Joel has mooved across the river some where in the
quaker settlement   he is agoing to run a breaking team   the team belongs to
him and Anderson and Hervy is going to help him run it   Mat Mount is at
home on a furlow but July Ann is gone   she run off with another man just
before Mat got home   she left the children with Mats father   we hant heard
sertain what was the cause of her leaveing but it is reported that her hide was
getting tight   Kate McCabe died some time ago   hant heard a word about the
sheep since last summer   I hant wrote wrote any thing about the wool to
Caldwel for I knew they would keep it til it is called for   if you hant went
home before you get this I think you had better stay down there til I get home
though I cant tel any thing about when that wil be   we cant get any news lately there is diferent rumors but nothing certain the 17" Corps left here this
morning but I dont know where they war going   it is reported that the terms
that war agreed on by Sherman and the rebel generels was not excepted by old
Andy   but I dont know whether it is true or not   you wil be likely to know
before you get this as I have nothing of importance to write I wil close for the

present and write some to to father and mother
with love I remain your affectionate husband as ever
William Coffin

I wil write again before we leave here if we dont start in the morning   if we
do you wil be able to hear where we are striking for write and direct as before
yours as ever

Dear father and Mother   I wil try to write you a few lines though I dont feel
that I have anything to write that wil be likely to interest you mutch   I suppose you would like to know some thing about Raleigh but if you war ever here
I expect you know about as mutch how it looks as I do   for it dont look as
though it had changed mutch in the last 40 years   I dont think it is as large a
place as Fairfield was the last I saw it though it is a diferent looking town
there a good many very large nice houses and many others verry poor   it is
inhabited at the present by a mixed mess of human being   they consist of
white citizens black citizens   yanks parolled rebels one armed and one
legged rebels & C

Raleigh N. C
April 27th 1865

My dear wife   I this evening take my pen to write you a few lines   I am wel
at present and I hope when this reaches you it may find you and the children
wel   I received your letter of the 8 th yesterday   I was glad to hear from
you again and to hear that you war all wel   I dont know why you dont get any
letters from me   I have wrote pretty often since we got to Goldsboro   I have
directed the letters to Pleasant Plain   you wrote that you dident aim to stay at
your fathers long and dident tel me to direct my letters there so I stil directed
to Pleasant Plain expecting you would go back there soon   we dident leave
here yesterday as was expected and I dont know when we wil   there is lots of
rumors but as there is nothing reliable I wont write anything about them you
done write in selling the colt if you was out of money and couldent hear from
me   I would rather have kept it if I could have made arrangement for you to
get money other ways in time   I sent you an order to get $25   I want you to
write whether you get it or not if you think you wil kneed it before I get home
you had better get it for I dont think we wil be paid til we are mustered out
you had better not buy any thing for house keeping only what you keed at present til I get home   I wrote to Nathan in the last letter   I wrote to you to take
Din to the best horse in the country   but for fear you dont get that letter I wil
write again   I want you to tel him to be shure and tend to it in time   no
more at present

I remain your husband as ever
Wm Coffin to R L C

near Petersburg Va
May 8th 1865

Dear wife I this morning take my pen to write you a few lines I am wel at present and hope this may find you all wel   we left Raleigh on the 29th of April and got here yesterday we marched very hard   the roads war good and the weather tolerable pleasant the most of the time a little to warm was the worst I dident march any til the two last days before we got here I took sick the day before we started and war sent to the Hospital the morning we started   I wasent mutch sick only one day   I had something like the cholera maybe   I feel as wel now as common   we are to lay over here today and then we wil go on to Richmond   I hant bin in Petersburg yet   we are camped over a mile from town   I hant seen any such works here yet as I have heard there was here I dont know how mutch farther we wil have to march   the talk is that we wil have to march to Washington or Alexandria   I guess they wil run us around til our time is out or at any rate we cant tel yet when we wil get done marching I received your letters of the 17th & 21st   one the day before we left Raleigh and the other the day after but I dident have time to answer til now   you wanted to know if I had any eggs for easter I dident have any   I have had just 3 eggs since we left Tenn over one year ago but we are begining to look forward to the time when we wil have the pleasure of eating sutch things again it is very comon to hear the boys talk how they wil eat when they get home   as I have nothing of importance to write I wil close and write a few lines to father and mother
I remain your husband as ever
Wm Coffin to R L Coffin
. Dear father & Mother   I wil try to write you a few lines   we dident get out in Gilford Co   I would like to have seen that country very wel and if we had have went that way   I would have went and seen Bennys father and as many of the rest of the connection as I could   wel mother thee said thee would like for me to be there to eat some of thy cooking   I would like it myself but I guess I wouldent be there long til thee would wish I was gone again   when ever thee goes to cooking for me thee wil find it like cooking for a log rolling   you must rase lots of garden stuff   if you want any for fall use   for I am to stay a week or so and unless you have lots I wil eat it all up   tel benny I would like to have seen his father and friends and I would like to have give his reb cousin his compliments if I could
I wil close for this time your son as ever
Wm Coffin

Near Manchester Va
May 12th 1865

Dear wife   I this evening take my pen to write you a few lines to let you know where we are and how I am getting along & C I am wel as common   the boys are all tolerable wel   we left Petersburg on tuesday and got here a wednesday   we are in 2 miles of Manchester and Richmond is just across the James River from Manchester   we wil start for Alexandria in the morning we can se Richmond from here very plain but I hant bin over in the town yet Petersburg is a nice town and a nice country around it   it has bin damaged slightly by our shelling but nothing to what I expected to se   the fortifications around Petersburg are not near as good as I expected to se   there is some strong works between Peters burg & Richmond   this is a nice country on the south of Richmond   you wil want to know when I think I wil get home I can tel you that there is no telling yet   we go from here to Alexandria   there the Army is to be reviewed commencing the 24" and probably it wil take a week and then it is thought we wil turn over our govenment property and and then as fast as we can get transportation we wil be sent to our own to be mustered out   it wil take some time to muster us out after we get to our own state on account of our officers being so behind with their books   they hant had their Co books with them since we left Rome and all the business from then til now wil have to be fixed up after they get their books   we have bin mooveing so much for the last six months that their books have never come to them yet   it is generally thought that we wil get home against the 1"of July but we cant tel it depends a goodeal on our luck about transportation   I am getting very anxious for the time to roll around so is all the boys   we had quite a storm last evening   there was 4 men killed by lightening in the 1 '' Division of our Corps   it rained all night and was cool this morning but has turned up more pleasant this aftnoon   we have had some mail since we came here but I have not got any I wrote to you at Petersburg but I forgot and directed it to Pleasant Plain   I have nothing mutch to write so I wil close for this time hopeing it wont be long til we can converse in a diferent and more pleasant way
I remain your husband as ever
Wm Coffin To Rachel L Coffin

Alexandria D C
May 21st 1865

Dear Wife   I this morning take my pen to write you a few lines   I am wel at present and hope this may find you and the children enjoying the same great blessing   we got here last evening   we are camped 2 miles west of Alexandria and about 6 miles from Washington City,   we can se the City from here   the Potomac River is between here and Washington   Shermans Army wil be reviewed wednesday the 24 th   we wil go over to Washington to be reviewed   we think our marching is about done though we may not get home for some time   it is reported that Sherman has issued orders for the men to put up quarters that wil do to stay in 6 weeks   our march from Richmond here was not very hard   we took it slow   we had some very warm weather which made it pretty hard   we have had a goodeal of rain for 2 days   it has bin raining all this morning   I got your letter of the 26" of April last evening   I was glad to hear from you and to hear that you war all well   I hant hant any letter from Anderson since I wrote to you before   Zeke Davis got back to the Co last evening we got to se Liby Prison and Castle thunder as we came through Richmond   they are pretty rusty looking places   there was a lot of Jonnys in Castle thunder reaping their reward for the way they used our prisners there   Richmond is a good sized place but there has bin a good lot of it burnt   there is a heap of the town that looks old and rusty but there is some good buildings in it.   as I have a very poor chance to write I wil close for the present for I dont expect you can read what I have wrote but if you cant you must excuse me for I have to write where I cant get up strait   I have to lay on my side and write   we have our shelter tents stretched rite on the ground so we can just lay in them and when it comes a rainy day like this so we cant be out we have to lay all the time   no more at present
I remain your husband as ever
Wm Coffin To Rachel L Coffin

Near Washington D C
May 25th 1865

Dear wife   I this evening take my pen to write you a few lines I am wel at present and hope this may find you wel   we crossed the Potomac River yesterday morning and pased in Review through the city and came out here and camped   we are about 3 miles N E of town   there was a great many spectators in town to witness the review.   everybody seemed anxious to see the Army every thing that could posibly be done was done to show that our services war fully appreciated   all the citizens have used us very kindly around

here   the report now is that the one years men and the 62 men wil be mustered out soon   I hope it wil be so it wil take some time to get the muster out rolls ready   I received your letters of the 15" a few days ago but I had just wrote so I thought I would wate a few days   I got a letter from Anderson wrote the 27" of April   he said he had rented all the place   Louis Macy Bill Davenport and Ike davis are tending it   they are all rather heavy purps but if they rase more than I can make use of maybe the railroad wil be close enough so I can ship it off Anderson wrote that he had sold the most of the corn   he said it was getting damaged and the rats was eating it pretty bad so he thought he had better sel it   I wil not try to describe things to you about the city as I couldent se things very wel as we passed though   I want to go down before we leave here and take a better view of things generally   as   I have nothing of mutch importance to write I wil close for this time
I remain your husband as ever
Wm Coffin To Rachel L Coffin

Washington City
June   2nd 1865

Dear wife   I this evening take my pen to write you a few lines to let you know that I am wel and I hope this wil find you and the children wel   I hant had arry letter from you since I wrote before   I cant tel you yet when we wil get away from here   we have to stay here til our officers get the muster out Rolls finished which wil be some time yet   they war behind so with their books that it takes a heap of work to get things stratened up   when we leave here we wil go to Davenport and there be paid off   I dont think we wil be detained mor than 3 or 4 days at Davenport   I cant tel when for you to look for me home but I expect to be there just as soon as I can   the weather is very warm here at the present the troops that dont come under the present order for mustering out are leaveing for Louisville all the time   our Division wil be likely to get away tomorrow   the 1st and 2nd Brigade left today as I have nothing of importance to write I wil close
I remain your husband as ever
Wm Coffin To Rachel L Coffin